Image Processing with ImageJ

Discover the incredible possibilities of ImageJ,
from basic image processing to macro and
plugin development

José María Mateos Pérez

Javier Pascau

PUBLISHING

BIRMINGHAM - MUMBAI

Image Processing with ImageJ

First published: September 2013

Production Reference: 1160913

Published by Packt Publishing Ltd.
Livery Place
35 Livery Street
Birmingham B3 2PB, UK..

ISBN 978-1-78328-395-8

www.packtpub.com

Cover Image by Aniket Sawant (aniket_sawant_photography@hotmail.com)

Credits

Authors

José María Mateos Pérez

Javier Pascau

Reviewers

Cristina Chavarrías

Ron DeSpain

Dr M Partridge

Acquisition Editor

Rubal Kaur

Commissioning Editor

Yogesh Dalvi

Technical Editor

Krishnaveni Haridas

Project Coordinator

Esha Thakker

Proofreader

Mario Cecere

Indexer

Monica Ajmera Mehta

Graphics

Abhinash Sahu

Production Coordinator

Shantanu Zagade

Cover Work

Shantanu Zagade

About the Authors

José María Mateos Pérez is a Spanish researcher and a Ph.D. student in the Medical Imaging Laboratory of the Hospital General Universitario Gregorio Marañón (`http://image.hggm.es`), in Madrid, where his main research lines deal with automatic segmentation and kinetic analysis modeling of dynamic nuclear imaging sequences. He has also been an experienced ImageJ user and has developed several macros and plugins. One of them, jClustering, has been published in PLOS ONE, a peer-reviewed journal. When he has enough time to procrastinate, he also likes to develop data analysis tools in Python and R.

> I would like to thank María for her support during the writing of this book. Also, I feel the need to mention The Army of Small Animals that live or lived in our house. They are a force for good.

Javier Pascau received his Ph.D. from Polytechnic University in Madrid, in 2006, and is currently a visiting professor at Carlos III University in Madrid. He has been a part of the Biomedical Imaging and Instrumentation Group, a research laboratory with a multidisciplinary team of engineers, physicists, biologists, and physicians located both in the university and Hospital General Universitario Gregorio Marañón, (`biig.uc3m.es`). His research and teaching cover areas such as medical image processing, analysis, quantification, and multimodal registration, both in preclinical and clinical environments. He has been involved in the development of small animal PET and CT devices, and in the last few years he has led several projects on intraoperative radiation therapy and image guided surgery. He has authored more than 30 papers, published in peer-reviewed journals over the last 13 years.

> I want to thank all my colleagues at the university and the hospital, since my knowledge on image processing is the result of multiple interactions in this multidisciplinary environment. Special thanks to my family and to my tireless coauthor, who has lead this common work.

About the Reviewers

Cristina Chavarrías is a telecommunications engineer specialized in medical imaging, in general, and **magnetic resonance imaging** (**MRI**), in particular. Her background reaches other imaging modalities and techniques such as nuclear imaging, computed tomography or spectroscopy, and ranges from data acquisition, preprocessing and correction to image processing. Despite being a junior researcher, she has been working for seven years in the Medical Imaging Laboratory at Hospital Gregorio Marañón, which offers a privileged view over the latest imaging challenges and allows direct contact with the clinical practice.

Ron DeSpain has been a physicist with over 45 years of experience working for major aerospace and defense companies. Ron has used ImageJ for advanced scientific algorithm development, since it was made available on Macintosh in the early 1990s. Since then it has been rewritten in Java and now runs on all major computers that support the Java virtual machine, making it his program of choice due to its powerful and versatile rapid development environment for signal imagery and video analysis applications. He has developed applications in intelligence analysis, missile guidance, target detection and recognition, 2D/3D imaging, automatic graph reading, remote sensing, sensor fusion, machine vision, image & video analysis, robotics, medical imaging, ultrasonic, x-ray, eddy current, and IR testing and manufacturing automation for more than 20 years.

Dr M Partridge did his BSc in biochemistry from Lancaster university before spending a number of years working for Mediwatch Biomedical, developing a range of point-of-care sensor systems. He then left Mediwatch to join the Cranfield University, where he obtained a Ph.D. in molecular coatings of fibre optic sensors and continued work as a researcher developing a number of optical sensors systems. Matthew's current research is focused on the development of optical sensors both biological applications such as point-of-care testing and industrial VOS sensor systems.

www.PacktPub.com

Support files, eBooks, discount offers and more

You might want to visit www.PacktPub.com for support files and downloads related to your book.

Did you know that Packt offers eBook versions of every book published, with PDF and ePub files available? You can upgrade to the eBook version at www.PacktPub.com and as a print book customer, you are entitled to a discount on the eBook copy. Get in touch with us at service@packtpub.com for more details.

At www.PacktPub.com, you can also read a collection of free technical articles, sign up for a range of free newsletters and receive exclusive discounts and offers on Packt books and eBooks.

http://PacktLib.PacktPub.com

Do you need instant solutions to your IT questions? PacktLib is Packt's online digital book library. Here, you can access, read and search across Packt's entire library of books.

Why Subscribe?

- Fully searchable across every book published by Packt
- Copy and paste, print and bookmark content
- On demand and accessible via web browser

Free Access for Packt account holders

If you have an account with Packt at www.PacktPub.com, you can use this to access PacktLib today and view nine entirely free books. Simply use your login credentials for immediate access.

Table of Contents

Preface

Welcome to *Image Processing with ImageJ*. Whether you are new to the world of image processing or an advanced researcher, we hope you will enjoy reading this book and find it useful for your analytic tasks.

The ImageJ imaging analysis software is becoming increasingly used among a vast array of different disciplines. As its user interface is far from a spectacular's view, a novel user may feel there are only a few things that this amazing program can add to its daily tasks. However, once the ImageJ basics are understood, it becomes a basic device in the toolbox of any scientist who needs to work with images on a daily basis.

This book covers briefly many basic image operations in ImageJ, and then proceeds to more complicated topics: advanced regions of interest delineation and management, filtering in spatial and frequency domains, or particle analysis.

One of the powers of ImageJ is the possibility of automating the different operations, so they can be replicated easily or applied to a large number of different images. This macro system is explained in detail through several exercises that help in showing the reader the potential of this system.

As ImageJ is a public domain software, many developers have contributed their own plugins in order to extend what ImageJ can do by itself. The last two chapters are dedicated to this topic from the perspective of the user who just wants to install new plugins, with a list consisting of our own selection, and also from the point of view of the developer who wants to use ImageJ as the platform to build powerful tools.

Independently of your background and objective, we hope this book has something for you.

What this book covers

Chapter 1, Getting Started with ImageJ, introduces the ImageJ image analysis platform and guides the reader through the installation process.

Chapter 2, Basic Image Processing with ImageJ, introduces the concept of digital image and the different types of data that ImageJ can handle, and then presents the intensity histogram and some basic image operations.

Chapter 3, Advanced Image Processing with ImageJ, describes more advanced imaging analysis techniques, such as modifying the pixel values of different images and performing local measurements. It also covers image filtering in the spatial and frequency domains.

Chapter 4, ImageJ Macros, presents one of the most powerful features of ImageJ: its macro system. Here we introduce this concept and show the reader how different operations can be automatized by giving several examples.

Chapter 5, ImageJ Plugins for Users, is used to explain how ImageJ can be extended very easily. There are literally hundreds of different plugins that extend its native features. In this chapter, we explain the ImageJ plugin system from the point of view of a user who does not necessarily need to know how to program. We perform a sample installation and list some plugins that we have found useful.

Chapter 6, ImageJ Plugins for Developers, is addressed for you if you are a developer. You might not just want to stop at using whatever plugins others have coded for you, but might want to try and implement your own algorithms. We explain briefly the ImageJ plugin architecture, the main classes that you will have to deal with, and how to integrate ImageJ with Eclipse, a very powerful Java IDE.

What you need for this book

There is not much material needed in order to follow this book. As ImageJ is a multi-platform public domain software package coded in Java, you just need a desktop computer or a laptop, optionally with the latest Java version installed. And if you don't have it, don't worry too much, as ImageJ can provide it for you.

In order to follow the last sections of the sixth chapter, you will also need the Eclipse IDE installed on your system. Please remember that this chapter is aimed at people with prior programming experience, so if that is not your case, you will not need it.

Also, you will probably need some images to keep practicing, apart from the ones we already provided, but that is up to you.

Who this book is for

This book is intended for everyone who does scientific work with images and is interested in knowing what can be achieved with ImageJ. The introductory part is a very broad introduction to the field of digital image processing, while the latter chapters are devoted to more complex analysis techniques in addition to an introduction to the macro and plugin system, that we hope will clarify these concepts to everyone interested in automating their analysis procedures or implementing their own image analysis algorithms. We have tried to accomplish a good balance between a step-by-step guide for non-advanced users and a nice introduction for developers who might want to use ImageJ as the development platform of their choice.

Conventions

In this book, you will find a number of styles of text that distinguish between different kinds of information. Here are some examples of these styles, and an explanation of their meaning.

Code words in text are shown as follows:

You can also send the .class files that will be placed in your plugins directory.

A block of code is set as follows:

```
run("Split Channels");
selectWindow("tuberculosis_full.tif (blue)");
close();
selectWindow("tuberculosis_full.tif (red)");
close();
selectWindow("tuberculosis_full.tif (green)");
run("Subtract Background...", "rolling=30");
```

New terms and **important words** are shown in bold. Words that you see on the screen, in menus or dialog boxes for example, appear in the text like this: "It can be done, as the error message states, by navigating to the **Options | Memory & Threads** command from the menu".

 Warnings or important notes appear in a box like this.

 Tips and tricks appear like this.

Reader feedback

Feedback from our readers is always welcome. Let us know what you think about this book—what you liked or may have disliked. Reader feedback is important for us to develop titles that you really get the most out of.

To send us general feedback, simply send an e-mail to feedback@packtpub.com, and mention the book title through the subject of your message.

If there is a topic that you have expertise in and you are interested in either writing or contributing to a book, see our author guide on www.packtpub.com/authors.

Customer support

Now that you are the proud owner of a Packt book, we have a number of things to help you to get the most from your purchase.

Downloading the example code

You can download the example code files for all Packt books you have purchased from your account at http://www.packtpub.com. If you purchased this book elsewhere, you can visit http://www.packtpub.com/support and register to have the files e-mailed directly to you.

Errata

Although we have taken every care to ensure the accuracy of our content, mistakes do happen. If you find a mistake in one of our books—maybe a mistake in the text or the code—we would be grateful if you would report this to us. By doing so, you can save other readers from frustration and help us improve subsequent versions of this book. If you find any errata, please report them by visiting http://www.packtpub.com/support, selecting your book, clicking on the **errata submission form** link, and entering the details of your errata. Once your errata are verified, your submission will be accepted and the errata will be uploaded to our website, or added to any list of existing errata, under the Errata section of that title.

Piracy

Piracy of copyright material on the Internet is an ongoing problem across all media. At Packt, we take the protection of our copyright and licenses very seriously. If you come across any illegal copies of our works, in any form, on the Internet, please provide us with the location address or website name immediately so that we can pursue a remedy.

Please contact us at `copyright@packtpub.com` with a link to the suspected pirated material.

We appreciate your help in protecting our authors, and our ability to bring you valuable content.

Questions

You can contact us at `questions@packtpub.com` if you are having a problem with any aspect of the book, and we will do our best to address it.

Getting Started with ImageJ

Welcome to the first chapter of *Image Processing with ImageJ*. **ImageJ** is public domain multi-platform software for image analysis written in the Java programming language. It includes predefined functions for a great variety of common tasks and can be extended easily using macros, scripting in several programming languages (including JavaScript and Python), and Java plugins.

In this brief introduction, you will read what ImageJ is, and how to install it, along with some minor configuration tricks. By the end of this chapter, you will have a working ImageJ installation in your system. Contents of this chapter include:

- A brief description of ImageJ and its main purpose
- An installation and upgrade guide
- How to tweak the amount of memory used by ImageJ, in case you are working with big images

ImageJ – history and motivation

 Readers who wish to read a more in-depth text about ImageJ's history should obtain the paper "NIH Image to ImageJ: 25 years of image analysis", published in Nature Methods, 2012, 9:7, pages 671-675.

ImageJ's development started as long ago as 1987, when it was not even named ImageJ and Java was yet to be born. That year, *Wayne Rasband* started coding a piece of software named "NIH Image" (after the National Institute of Health (USA), which funded his efforts) in order to provide a way to perform image analysis on the old Apple Macintosh II, which lacked an image analysis platform, and was starting to be the desktop system of choice for many scientists. He started distributing his software for free to anyone who requested it.

This imaging software became increasingly popular, but at the time the market for Apple computers was being surpassed by the PC. NIH Image was developed specifically for Apple systems and didn't work on the Windows platform. In 1995, the Java programming language was created by Sun Microsystems. This allowed Wayne to start porting his software so it would work on PCs, and at the same time maintain a single, multi-platform version of the source code. ImageJ was born.

During the development process, a great deal of care was taken to allow users to extend ImageJ's native capabilities with the help of macros that can be developed even by users with no prior programming experience; and an open API allowed experienced programmers to code their own plugins. This is one of the reasons for ImageJ's success among scientists that work with images regularly, along with the huge amount of macros and plugins available from the web page. At the time of this writing, the ImageJ's user mailing list had more than 2000 subscribers and is a very active discussion meeting point for everything related to this software and related projects.

What ImageJ is for (and what it is not for)

If you perform a search for "imagej" on some popular academic databases (such as PubMed (http://www.ncbi.nlm.nih.gov/pubmed), IEEE Xplore (http://ieeexplore.ieee.org/), or Google Scholar (http://scholar.google.com), you will find that this software has been successfully used in a huge number of scientific papers in fields that span several disciplines, from confocal microscopy to X-ray analysis, vehicle license plate detection, ultrasound diagnosis of breast cancer, development of automatic 4D segmentation algorithms or tomographic image reconstruction, to cite just a small sample.

ImageJ is not intended to serve as a replacement for Adobe Photoshop, GIMP, or any other graphics editing program. It is less centered on *layers, transparencies, cloning, or blurring*, and more on *quantification, filtering, measuring,* and *mathematical processing*. This does not mean that an image cannot be modified using ImageJ, but the type of modification that ImageJ is intended to do is of a different nature than that of the programs mentioned previously.

Installing ImageJ

ImageJ is software written in the Java programming language. In order to run it, **Java Runtime Environment** (from now on, just Java) should be installed in your system (go to `http://java.com` for more information). If you do not have it installed and cannot do it for any reason, you can download several ImageJ packages that include it, but the download size will be considerably larger. The current stable version of ImageJ (1.46r at the time of this writing, though the development is fast and new versions are released almost on a weekly basis) can be downloaded from: `http://imagej.nih.gov/ij/download.html`. The exact package to be downloaded depends on your particular situation (what operating system are you using, whether you have administrator privileges to perform a system-wide installation, and so on).

Depending on your particular needs, you may want to download the platform-specific installer package, or simply the platform-independent version that consists of a ZIP file, that can be uncompressed and run from your user directory, or even from a USB stick. The platform-specific packages are straightforward to use and behave just like a regular application for the operating systems they are built for; there is extensive documentation regarding the particular details of the installation process for each system in the main ImageJ webpage (Windows: `http://imagej.nih.gov/ij/docs/install/windows.html`; Linux: `http://imagej.nih.gov/ij/docs/install/linux.html`; Mac OS: `http://imagej.nih.gov/ij/docs/install/osx.html`). In the next subsections, we will talk a bit about performing a local installation with the platform-independent file. Depending on your particular configuration, you might want to use these files, as they do not require you to have administrative privileges, and allow you to install ImageJ in any folder in your user directory.

Windows

Download the file `ij146.zip` (or the one currently being offered) from the download page and unzip it to the folder where ImageJ will be installed. Inside the `ImageJ/` folder, double-click on `ImageJ.exe`. The following dialog will pop up:

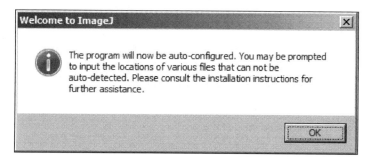

The auto-configuration process is pretty straightforward, and consists basically of detecting the path to your Java installation. If the path cannot be automatically found, you will be asked to provide the location of the `javaw.exe` file. Once this has been done, a new `ImageJ.cfg` file will be created in the directory where you have unzipped the file, and ImageJ will start. This file is created only in Windows. From that point on, double clicking on `ImageJ.exe` runs ImageJ, and a direct shortcut can be created on the desktop or where it is useful for your purposes.

Linux / Mac OS

Just like with the Windows version, download the `ij146.zip` (or the most current) file. Unzip it to the desired folder and execute the `run` script (on Mac systems, you can also double-click on the application icon). This file just contains a call to the Java virtual machine with the necessary parameters, so the `java` command needs to be in the system path; in this case, there is no Java autodetection or `ImageJ.cfg` generation. You can safely delete `ImageJ.exe`, as it is a Windows-only file.

First run

If everything has gone smoothly, you will see the main ImageJ window.

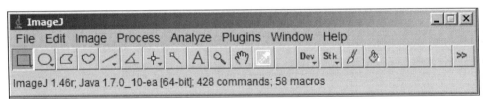

The main ImageJ window shown right after the first execution. Notice both the ImageJ version and the Java version on the status line at the bottom.

The status line shows that we are running **ImageJ 1.46r** using **Java 1.7.0** update 10 in a 64-bit system. Everything is ready for you to start processing images, but there are a couple of aspects that can be improved.

Updating the installation

As you can see on the ImageJ **News** webpage, new versions appear quite regularly. For this book, we installed version 1.46r, but we wanted to catch up with version 1.47q. This latest ImageJ version has new functionalities and bug fixes that may be interesting for the user. Fortunately, ImageJ has an internal update command that will allow you to perform the update process easily, and without any user intervention. Simply run the **Help | Update ImageJ...** command and you will get the following dialog:

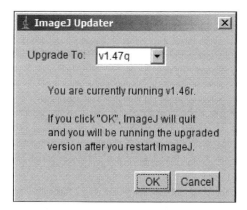

As you can see, it allows us to upgrade to the latest release and to other older versions, and bleeding-edge daily builds that are of no interest here. If you click on **OK**, your ImageJ installation will be upgraded and then automatically closed. The new version will be used the next time you run it.

 When you do it at home, the version number will surely be different. Do not worry! If there is a more recent version, just update to it. It may happen that you already have the most up-to-date version. In that case, you do not need to do anything.

Configuration options

Once you have a working ImageJ installation, you might want to tweak some configuration options, such as the appearance, font size, and proxy settings. These options are easily modified using the menus **Edit | Options | Fonts...**, **Edit | Options | Appearance...**, and **Edit | Options | Proxy Settings...**.

The next section is dedicated to explain how to tweak the one configuration parameter that might be vital during your analysis tasks: the amount of system memory available to ImageJ.

Memory limit increase

If you run **Help | About ImageJ...** you will get this nice image:

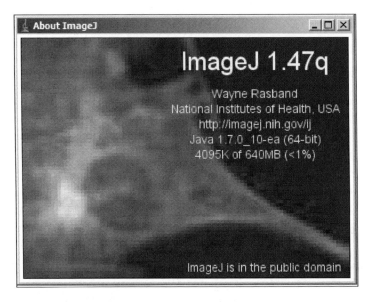

Along with the version (note the upgrade!), the information of ImageJ's main author, and some other data that resembles those previously commented, you can see that 4095 KB of RAM memory is used, from a total of 640 MB (less than 1 percent). Every time you open a new image, the amount of memory being used increases, until the limit is reached. Once you get to this point, an error will pop up, as ImageJ will not have the necessary resources. The error will be something like this:

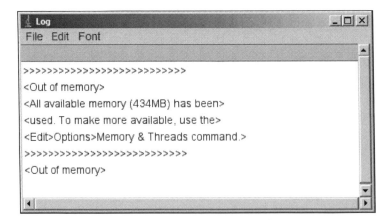

If you are going to work with big images, or you need to keep open a great number of them, it is wise to increase the memory limit for your system. It can be done, as the error message states, by navigating to the **Options | Memory & Threads** command from the menu. This will open the following dialog:

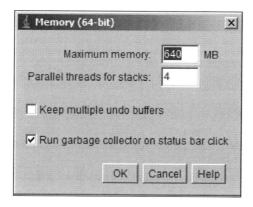

Here, you can select the total amount of memory you want ImageJ to use. For example, we change the **Maximum memory** field to a value of 2048, and click on **OK**. A new window will inform us that ImageJ will use the new limit upon restart.

In Windows systems, this value is stored in the Image.cfg file. Another option is to edit that file before running ImageJ. These are the contents of that file in a regular installation, though the exact path may vary:

```
C:\Program Files\Java\jre7\bin\javaw.exe
-Xmx640m -cp ij.jar ij.ImageJ
```

As you can see, this is just a call to the Java Runtime Environment with the appropriate parameters to run ImageJ. -Xmx640m defines the amount of memory available for the Java virtual machine. If we change that value to -Xmx2048m, we will accomplish the same result as before. This way of changing the total amount of memory can also be used in Linux; in this case, the value is stored in the run script as another argument for the Java virtual machine. These are the typical contents of the run script upon installation:

```
java -Xmx512m -jar ij.jar
```

This script just calls the java executable with the configured memory limits, and launches the application inside the ij.jar file. This memory limit can be changed directly in the script file.

Bear in mind that, for memory amounts bigger than 2 GB, a 64-bit system and appropriate Java version is needed.

 It is not a good idea to give ImageJ all the available memory. Your operating system and other programs need their share too.

Summary

In this chapter, you have learned what ImageJ is, and how it can be downloaded and installed. Now, you are ready for basic image processing concepts and examples detailed in the next chapter. For further reference, you are encouraged to visit the **ImageJ Information and Documentation** portal at `http://imagejdocu.tudor.lu/`, which complements the information provided in the official webpage.

2

Basic Image Processing with ImageJ

If you followed the instructions found in the preceding chapter, you will have a working ImageJ installation on your system. This chapter includes:

- Open and save images (from disk and from the ImageJ sample repository)
- Zoom on the image and obtain pixel values
- Color, multichannel, and stack images
- Adjusting your image brightness, contrast, and image size
- Thresholding

Image reading/writing

In this section, we learn how to open and write different images.

Opening images with a certain format

First of all, we will need an image to open. For this first exercise, we are going to use one of the several public domain images showing the "happy face" on Mars. Go to `http://www.msss.com/msss_images/2008/01/31/index.html` and download the image you see (`happy_face.jpg`, image credit to NASA / JPL / Malin Space Science Systems). Store it on your hard disk in a place that is easy to access, as you shall need it right away.

Now run ImageJ, execute **File | Open...**, and select the file you just downloaded. ImageJ will load the image contents into a new window and you should see something like this:

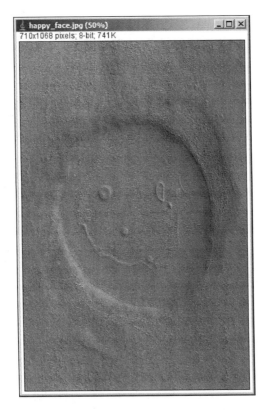

You just opened your first image using ImageJ. Smile!

We have scaled the image to fit in the page (note the **(50%)** on the title bar; more on this later), so your window will be bigger. In any case, you can check some common elements to all images opened in ImageJ.

- **Image title**: In this case, `happy_face.jpg`, which by default is the name of the file. This value is useful in order to know which image you are selecting for a specific processing step, or when you are dealing with macros. You can change it using **Image | Rename...**.

- **Information text about the image properties (Metadata)**: In this case, **710x1068 pixels; 8-bit; 741K**; these numbers indicate the dimensions of the image, in pixels (width * height), the number of bits per pixel, and the total amount of memory used by the image.

- The image itself displayed.

Let's stop for a while on the second point. A digital image is just a matrix containing numbers which are then represented on a computer screen as different gray values (as in this case) or a color scale. A single cell of that matrix is called a pixel; the dimensions of the image are the dimensions of the matrix in pixels. In this case, the image is contained within a matrix of 710 pixels wide and 1068 pixels high.

The number of bits per pixel indicates how the intensity values have been coded. An 8-bit image can store 256 different levels of intensity ($2^8 = 256$). The more bits per pixel an image uses, the more intensity levels we can store, but the image will need more disk or memory space. ImageJ handles the following image data types:

- **8 bits (unsigned integers)**: It consists of values from 0 to 255.

- **16 bits (unsigned integers)**: It comprises values from 0 to 65,535.

- **32 bits (real numbers)**: It handles floating point values.

- **8 bits color**: It uses a **lookup table (LUT)** to convert each gray level to a RGB triplet.

- **24/32 bits color**: It uses RGB values, every channel with 8 bits per pixel and an optional extra 8 bits for the alpha/transparency layer.

Now, the space occupied by the image is always a measure of how much memory is used. If an image has P pixels and each pixel takes up B bits, then it will need P * B bits of the RAM memory. In the case of the "happy face", this size would be 710 * 1068 * 8 = 6066240 bits; dividing by 8 we get 758280 bytes, and dividing by 1024 (that is the number of bytes in one KB) we obtain 741 KB, exactly as ImageJ displays. However, if we check the file size on disk, it takes 702 KB. Why this (small) discrepancy? Why is the image using more space on ImageJ than on our computer's hard disk? Some image formats (such as JPG which was used to encode this image) allow compressing the data so it takes less space on disk. In this case, the compression level is small, but much bigger ratios can be achieved, especially if we are willing to lose some information in exchange for less disk space.

ImageJ reads the following image formats natively, JPG, PNG, TIFF, BMP, GIF, DICOM, PGM, and FITS; the first ones are the most common. TIFF is the preferred format in ImageJ, because it is the one that can store several non-image properties as metadata (including regions of interest). DICOM is the standard format used for medical imaging, and FITS is typically used for astronomy data. These image formats are the ones that ImageJ can open natively, but there are several plugins that will allow it to open many other different formats. Please refer to the *Chapter 5, ImageJ Plugins for Users* for more information on this.

Another functionality ImageJ offers is the possibility of reading images stored in a text file as a 32-bit image. These images are stored in a tabbed format, and the number of rows and columns will define the final dimensions of the image. You can convert an image to this format using **Image | Transform | Image to Results** (and **Image | Transform | Results to Image** works the other way around).

Reading raw data

If your image data is stored in a proprietary format, or as binary data (for instance, if it is the result of some measures done using different software, and stored directly to disk), you may open it with the **File | Import | Raw....** menu option:

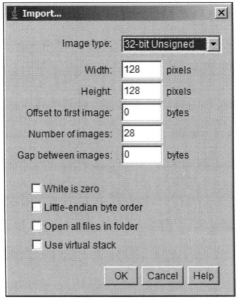

Dialog for importing raw images

A raw image is simply a sequence of values stored in a file that may be mixed with some header information. If you know how these values are ordered in the file, you can successfully load the image. As you can see in the previous interface, you will need to provide the data type of the stored values, image dimensions (**Width**, **Height**, and **Number of images**), **Offset to first image** (number of bytes of non-image data before the image values start in the file), and **Gap between images** (number of bytes of non-image data after the end of each image, before the start of the next one). You can select some specific features using the checkboxes.

As you have seen, importing raw images is a powerful feature, but the user needs to have lots of information regarding how the values have been stored on the file, and the total amount of images to open (for stacks). If the wrong values are provided, it is still possible to open the image, but it will display in erroneous ways (for instance, just part of the image is opened, or the pixel values are scrambled, or the image is replicated several times… the particular effect depends on the particular details of the data you need to open, and the parameter that has been incorrectly set). All this information is contained in the image file when a supported format is read, so in most cases you won't need to worry about it.

We could have also opened the "happy face" image by dragging-and-dropping it over the main ImageJ window, or by copying the URL, and using the **File | Import | URL...** menu option. Dragging-and-dropping is also a fast method to open folders with several images as stacks.

Online sample images

In this book, we will be using two groups of sample images to illustrate the different concepts that will be presented:

- ImageJ comes with several sample images that can be accessed from **File | Open Samples**. If we browse to that menu option, we can see different image modalities and formats listed. These images are stored in the NIH servers, and are downloaded from their remote location every time they are opened; please check if you can open any of them. If you are going to need them for offline access, a ZIP file that contains them can be downloaded from http://imagej.nih.gov/ij/download/sample-images.zip.

- We also provide some example images with the book, which can be downloaded from the Packt site. We will refer to these images as "test images".

One of the test images is named `tuberculosis_sample.tif`. Open it using the **File | Open...** (*Ctrl + O*), and you will obtain the following window:

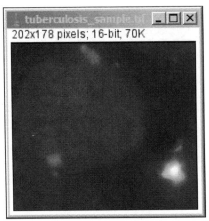

tuberculosis_sample.tif file opened in ImageJ

Saving images

Finally, suppose you have performed some analysis on a given image and want to store the results. This is as easy as running **File | Save As...** and selecting the appropriate format, which will depend on what are you going to use the image for (saving for posterior analysis will require a format with maximum quality like TIFF, while for web publication losing quality with JPG can be acceptable in exchange for small file size). When in doubt, select a format that uses lossless compression which will allow you to open the image exactly as you left it, such as TIFF.

Zooming on the image and pixel values

Let's stick with the image we just opened for a while, as it will be a good template for the next exercise. If we want to zoom in or out of a given image, we can run the **Image | Zoom | In [+]** and **Image | Zoom | Out [-]** menu options. It is much easier to use the shortcuts, (+) and (-). The current zoom level is added to the image title bar if it is different from 100 percent (recheck the figure shown when we opened `happy_face.jpg`, and you will find the zoom level set to **50%**). Now we can try zooming in and out of the `tuberculosis_sample.tif` file; the position of the mouse pointer on the image helps guiding the zoom in operation, since it is used to center the scaling. When the zoom level is too big, the main window stops getting bigger and the image is cropped. Two purple squares help the user keep track of the location inside the image. When this zoom level has been reached, you can keep the space bar pressed and drag the image around.

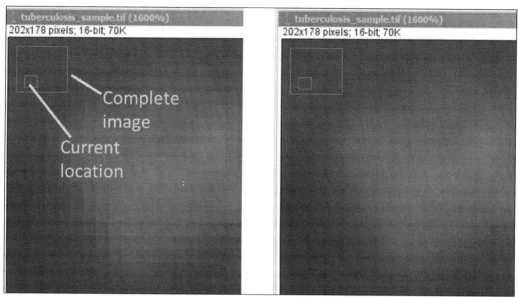

Zoomed image displayed when Interpolate zoomed images option is unchecked (left), and checked (right). Detail of the zoom guide overimposed on the image. Note the zoom level (1600 percent) on the title bar.

When an image is zoomed in, individual pixels will be displayed (left screenshot) or interpolated (right screenshot) depending on the **Interpolate zoomed images** option value available in the **Edit | Options | Appearance...** menu.

You can always check the values of the individual pixels that make up your image. When you move the mouse pointer over the image, ImageJ will show the corresponding image coordinates and pixel value in the status bar (below the menu and the toolbar). The image coordinates are measured in pixels, or whatever unit has been indicated in the image metadata. The spatial units can be set using **Analyze | Set Scale....** This way, you can indicate a specific distance in pixels (if you have created a **Straight line** with the corresponding tool, its pixel length will be automatically loaded), and the corresponding spatial measure (in mm for instance). Now, every time you move over the image, the "x" and "y" coordinates will be measured using that unit. Pixel intensities follow a similar convention. They can be calibrated for your image, or you may indicate which pixel intensities correspond to whatever intensity units you may use (optical density, radiotracer concentration...) using the **Analyze | Calibrate** menu.

In order to better understand how all this works, open the sample image named CT (the `ct.dcm.zip` file) that corresponds to a DICOM file (a format used for medical imaging). This image is scaled in spatial dimension and calibrated in pixel intensities. When you move the mouse over it, you will see the "x" and "y" coordinates in mm, the calibrated pixel value, and the original pixel value stored in the file in parentheses:

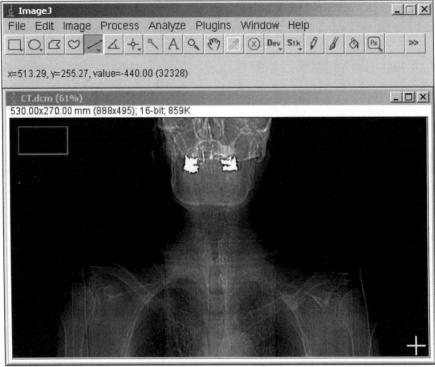

Sample image CT.dcm showing the coordinates (in millimeters, as the image is calibrated) and pixel value of the current cursor position (white cross at the bottom right).

If you want to see not only the current pixel but the values in a surrounding area, use the tool called **Pixel Inspector** using the **More Tools** icon (the double red arrow at the rightmost side of the toolbar). It provides a lot of information that can be even exported to an external file.

Color and multichannel images

Color images can be manipulated in different ways in ImageJ. The most basic option would be to use a pseudo color image, which is an 8-bit image in which every intensity value has a corresponding RGB color, resulting in 256 colors. This color mode is called pseudo color or false color because the color correspondence can be manually changed, depending on the color palette (or the Lookup Table) that we select. The GIF image format stores 8-bit images with the color palette included, so when we open a file in this format it will be displayed in color, although values for every pixel will be limited to 256 possibilities. Open the `tuberculosis_sample.gif` file again using the **File | Open** menu option. Now navigate to **Image | Lookup Tables**. In this menu, many LUTs are offered to be selected. Choose the one named **Fire** and the result will be:

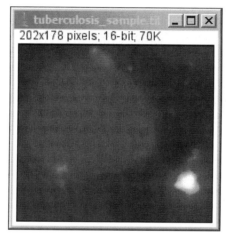

16-bit image with a Lookup Table applied (Fire LUT)
in order to display it with pseudo color

We can apply an 8-bit LUT to a 16-bit image. The pixel values are converted so that the original black is 0 and the original white is 255, and then the selected LUT is applied. You could also modify the current LUT from **Image | Color | Edit LUT...**.

Pseudo color is a nice solution, because when you display a grayscale image with certain LUTs, your visual system perceives intensity differences better. But in many cases, you will want to work with images containing True Color information, which means 24 bits RGB values. Every basic color component (Red, Green, or Blue) is quantized with 256 possible values (8 bits), which results in 2^24 (16,777,216) possible colors. When you open an image that stores RGB values (for instance, most JPG files) and then move the mouse cursor over it, ImageJ status bar will display the three values separated by commas. You can open the sample image named `Cardio.dcm` and check that there are three values stored for every pixel.

When you work with RGB images, the color information is commonly meaningful, and manipulating this information may be an interesting process. For instance, if an area of the image is red or green, it could mean something depending on the way you obtained your image. RGB images do not allow independent processing of every color channel. Multichannel or composite images are designed for this, the main advantage being that every channel is kept separated, so any measure will be done only on one of them. Multichannel images are not limited to 8 bits per channel, since R, G, and B are single images with 8, 16, or 32-bit depth types. All these features can be observed opening the test image named `tuberculosis.tif`. This image belongs to a microscopy study of auramine-stained samples of tissues potentially infected with tuberculosis bacilli, and is a composition of three channels, R, G, and B, each coded with 8 bits.

The slider at the bottom of the image window is used to select which channel we want to work with, and the pixel values in the status bar will correspond to that channel. The image description below the window title will also describe the channel selected with the slider. If we run **Analyze | Measure** (*Ctrl + M*), we will see some measurements shown in another window and these results will relate to the current channel. If we now use the slider at the bottom of the image to select the green channel, and repeat the **Analyze | Measure** command, the new line in the **Results** window would be measured on that channel.

The values shown in the **Results** window may vary depending on the particular parameters selected in the **Analyze | Set Measurements...** dialog.

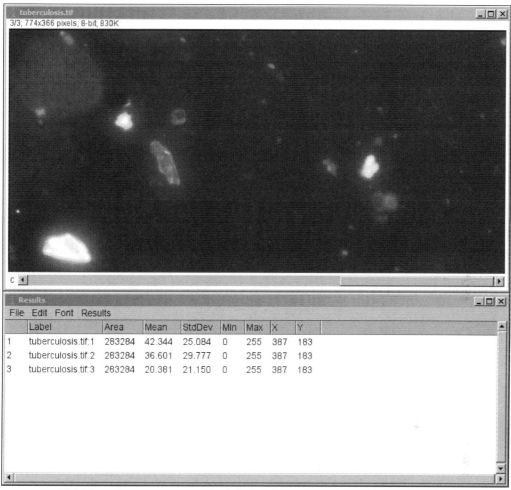

Multichannel microscopy image loaded in ImageJ (top) and Results window (bottom).
The measurements have been made with the slider selecting a different channel every time,
so each mean gray value is different in each Results table row.

More operations can be performed on the composite or RGB color images. Many of them are available from **Image | Color | Channels Tool...** (*Ctrl + Shift + Z*). From that interface, we can select which channels to display, show every channel as grayscale, convert a composite image to RGB (24 bits) type, split the channels creating three single images, or convert a RGB image to a composite image.

RGB images are not the only color model that ImageJ can handle. **Hue, Saturation, Brightness (HSB)** color model can be a more convenient representation in some situations, since brightness corresponds to the intensity information from the RGB image (R + G + B) / 3, and hue and saturation are closer to our conventional description of the colors as we perceive them (different reds correspond to the same hue and can be more or less saturated). If we want to work with this color model, we can convert any RGB image to a HSB stack from the **Image | Type** menu. If you are unsure about what color schema your image is using, the type menu option will tell you by displaying a tick next to the current image type.

Multichannel images have been our first contact with data of more than two dimensions. Now that we are familiar with these concepts, let's improve the possibilities and the number of dimensions in the following section.

3D and 4D images – stacks and hyperstacks

Digital images are not only bidimensional (2D) or multichannel (2D with several channels). We may have several 2D images with spatial, temporal, or any kind of relationship between them. These kinds of images are managed by ImageJ as stacks and hyperstacks. Stacks have three spatial dimensions: x, y, and z. Hyperstacks have four dimensions (x, y, z, and time) and both may also have several channels. As you may be thinking, these two kinds of images are really powerful, since almost any kind of single experiment that provides image results which are somehow related can be handled with them. Now, every image position is not a pixel but a **voxel** (it has volume), and has three or more dimensions. There is no need that all the dimensions are different from one, and consequently stacks are a subgroup of hyperstacks.

Let's open one sample stack to start familiarizing with this concept. Open the sample image described as T1 head (file t1-head.zip). This stack corresponds to a Magnetic Resonance Imaging (MRI) acquisition of a patient's head, so every 2D image is a slice showing the internal anatomy. You can move slice by slice with the arrow keys or your mouse wheel, or automatically by clicking on the small play icon in the bottom left of the image window (by right-clicking on the same icon, animation options can be accessed). **Image | Show info...** (*Ctrl + I*) displays the metadata information from the image file, providing details on the image acquisition as free text. To display the scale in every dimension, navigate to **Image | Properties...** (*Ctrl + Shift + P*) and you will see the window shown in the right-hand side of the following screenshot:

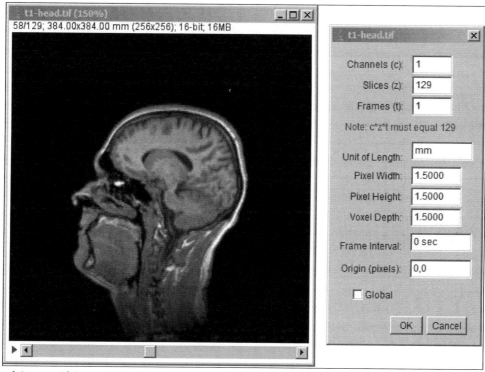

Stack image with Image Properties window on the right. The 2D dimensions are shown in the image window (256x256), and the current slice on the left is number 58 out of 129. The scaling for every dimension is shown in the properties window (on the right).

All images in the stack must have the same 2D dimensions. ImageJ uses pixel width, height, and voxel depth as scaling factors to convert voxel coordinates into mm (as in this image, the unit of length is mm), and show them as usual on the status bar.

So now that we understand the basic concepts on stacks, let's start playing with them. The fact that we now have three dimensions will allow lots of processing steps to be applied to these images. You will find most operations available in the **Image | Stacks** menu. The first operation you will find, deals with adding or deleting slices. When you add a slice, it is placed after the current one in the stack and it is filled with background intensity, and when you choose to delete a slice, the current one will be removed from your stack; the "z" dimension will be updated in both cases. You can move forwards and backwards slice by slice from this menu and also go to a specific slice number.

If for any reason you want to convert your nice 3D stack into a set of 2D individual images, you can do it easily with **Image | Stacks | Stack to Images**. If you try to do this with the previously opened sample (T1 head), ImageJ will warn you because creating 129 images (in their corresponding windows) may not be a good idea. The inverse operation is also available (**Image | Stacks | Images to Stack**), which is useful in case you have different 2D images that could in fact be processed together as a stack. If you need to do this with a large number of images, you may place all your 2D individual images in the same folder, with the desired slice number in every file name, and drag-and-drop the folder in ImageJ status bar. ImageJ will read all images in the folder, sort them according to the file names, and create a stack. Afterwards, you can introduce scaling for every dimension and other parameters using **Image | Properties** (*Ctrl + Shift + P*).

Moving through the slices of a stack using the scrolling bar is a good way to explore your data, but sometimes it can be convenient to present all your 3D data in a single image. **Image | Stacks | Make Montage...** will help you in this process. The following screenshot depicts this process on our T1 head sample stack:

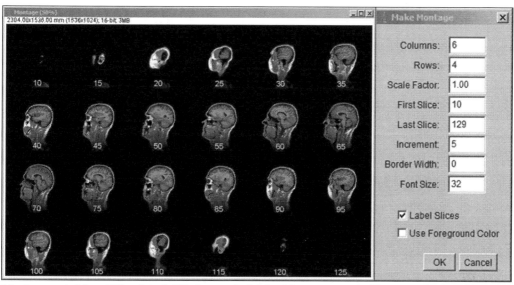

Montage created from T1 head stack. Window on the left is a Montage created with options shown on the right.

Since this stack has 129 slices, we have modified the Montage options to display a grid with **6** columns and **4** rows, starting on slice number **10** (the first 9 slices were almost black), and including in the Montage, one of each five slices (**Increment = 5**). If **Label Slices** is checked (as in our example) you will see the slice label overimposed. We have modified the default **Font Size** to a larger value in order to display the labels correctly (**Font Size = 32**). All these values are not the ones that ImageJ fills in when you open the Montage interface for the T1 head image, so it can be a good exercise for you to modify them and see how different Montages are created.

All those 2D images integrated as a stack are, therefore, a 3D matrix of data, with an intensity value for every matrix position or voxel. Because of this, the 2D images that are displayed in the previous example are one possible way of reading your data, the 2D image is created reading "x" and "y" positions with a fixed "z" value. But if for instance, we fix the "x" coordinate and create a new 2D images reading "y" and "z" positions, we will be creating slices that are orthogonal to the ones in Montage. This can be done using **Image | Stacks | Reslice...** (/).You will need to select the direction of your new slicing (starting at left, top...) and the spacing of your new slices. When you click on **OK**, ImageJ will create a new stack with the desired orientation.

Reslicing probably has helped you in understanding the concept of stacks as 3D images. But it is a static process; you describe the new slicing, create a new stack, and done. With the same concept, but implemented in an interactive way, you can explore your 3D data. This option is accessed from **Image | Stacks | Orthogonal Views** (*Ctrl + Shift + H*), and is something commonly available at medical workstations:

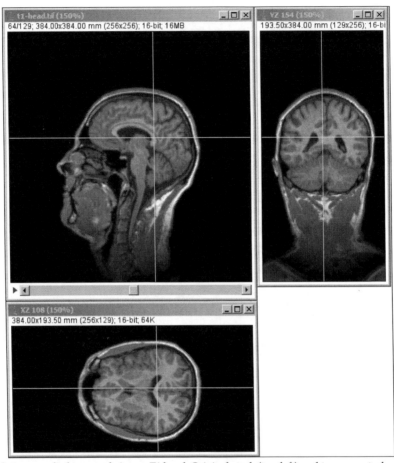

Orthogonal views applied to sample image T1 head. Original stack (top-left) and two new stacks created from the original in XY (bottom), and YZ (top right) directions are synchronized, so every time the user clicks on any of them the yellow axes are moved to that position, and the other two windows update.

As you can see in the screenshot, when you apply this operation on a stack, two new windows are created, that would be the result of reslicing the image in two orthogonal directions to the one originally shown in the stack. The new feature that this tool presents is that the three views are synchronized, so every time you click on a certain position, the other two windows update their slices to the corresponding coordinate (the yellow axis cross in the example).

Another processing that we can perform on our stack is 3D projection. You can think of it as a series of rays that will pass through your 3D volume and intersect a virtual 2D screen on the other side. You will be able to modify the orientation of this projection and the way these rays interact with your volume. You can just average all values of the volume intersected by every ray, calculate the maximum value, and keep the value that is closer to the 2D screen. Depending on the kind of projection, a different result is obtained. **Image | Stacks | Z Project...** will run this process only once, in the direction perpendicular to your slices, calculating the projected value (**Average Intensity**, **Max Intensity**, **Min Intensity**…) from all slices. The result will be a single 2D image.

Image | Stacks | 3D Project... allows modifying more options and calculates several projections rotating your stack around one of the main axes 360 degrees (default value, though it can be changed). The result is a new stack that when animated (with the play button at the bottom left of the image window), presents your rendered projections one after the other. This nice result can be saved as an AVI movie (**File | Save As | AVI...**) and is an interesting way of exploring your stacks. Test it with the `T1 head` image, selecting **Mean Value** as **Projection Method** and leaving the remaining options unmodified. Your result should be the same as in the following diagram, where the whole 3D projection process is illustrated:

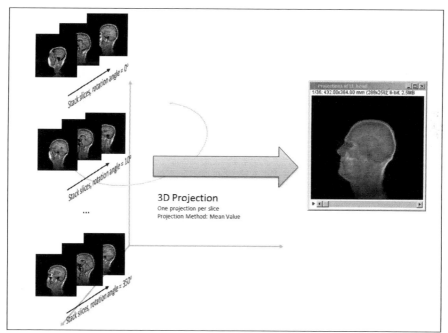

The scheme of 3D projection process is shown. In this example, the stack is rotated 10 degrees around the y axis, and in every rotation the projection calculates the average value and obtains a 2D image. All these images together (total of 36, one every 10 degrees) are the result (right of the diagram), that is also a stack and can consequently be animated.

As you have seen in this section, we have focused about stacks, and almost nothing has been said on hyperstacks. This is because the way you interact with hyperstacks and stacks is similar, taking into account that hyperstacks have more dimensions (time and channels). Some of the operations that you can apply to stacks can also be applied to hyperstacks, and if that is not possible, ImageJ will show a warning message. The only specific tools that you will find in the **Image** | **Hyperstacks** menu are those related to type conversion, such as converting stacks to hyperstacks and one tool to reduce dimensionality, that will create a new hyperstack fixing the position, time frame, or channel that you select.

To better understand how hyperstacks are manipulated, open the sample image called Mitosis. This image has 2 channels, 5 slices, and 51 frames, so it is a great example of complex data, and we encourage you to try it and move around all you need until you feel comfortable with the different dimensions. Also, create the **Orthogonal Views** (*Ctrl + Shift + H*) using the option on the **Image** | **Stacks** menu, and move around with them.

There is an option in case you want to process large images (for instance, hundreds of megabytes). You can open them as Virtual Stacks. In that case, the whole image will not be loaded in memory, but it will be accessed from disk, loading only the part of the stack or hyperstack that is needed. This is slower, but it will allow you to process images that do not fit in your system memory.

Image adjust tools

In this section, we will explore different tools that can be used for basic image processing.

Image histogram and window/level parameters

In this section, we will first understand one basic descriptor of the image intensity content, the image histogram. It will allow us to better understand what the intensity processing tools are doing. The image histogram is a graphical representation of the intensity values present in the image that plots the number of pixels for each intensity value. It shows intensity distribution over the image at a glance, and will help a lot when adjusting the way these intensities are displayed or modified.

Histograms, like most of the concepts in this book, are better understood with examples. Open two test images: `happy_face.jpg` and `tuberculosis_sample.tif`. If you look at these images side-by-side, you will notice that the intensity distributions are quite different, that is, `happy_face` presents a similar intermediate intensity along the image (gray pixels), with almost no dark or bright areas, while `tuberculosis_sample` has large areas with low intensity (dark pixels), and some high intensity spots (bright pixels). Now we will take a look at the histograms of every image. Select each image window and run **Analyze | Histogram** (*H*). A new histogram window is created for every image; this window shows a plot representing the intensity levels in the horizontal axis (from 0 to 255 in these images), and the number of pixels for each intensity level in the vertical axis:

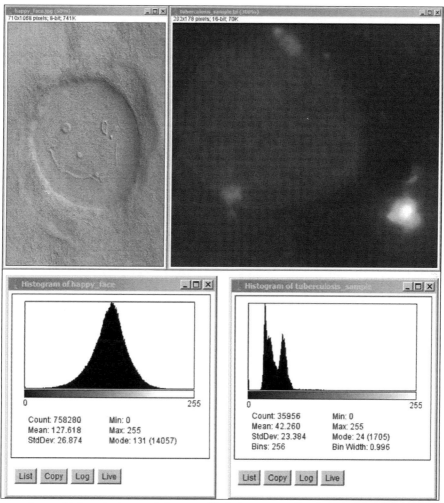

happy_face and tuberculosis_sample images with their corresponding histograms. Note that, as the tuberculosis image is a 16-bit image, the pixel values have been grouped (Bins: 256).

For every histogram, descriptive statistics are shown: mean, standard deviation, mode, minimum, and maximum. Notice that the value labeled as count corresponds to the summation of all values for every intensity value, and consequently corresponds to the total number of pixels in every image (for instance, the image `happy_face` has 710 * 1068 = 758280 pixels, which is the count value for its histogram). When you move the mouse pointer over the histogram, the intensity and the pixel count (the value of the histogram, for that intensity) corresponding to that position are displayed.

Now, let's take a look at the shape of these two histograms. For the image `happy_face`, the majority of the pixels have intermediate intensity values (different shades of gray in the image). This is represented in the histogram as one mode, one peak, surrounded by high histogram values. The histogram shows low values at the beginning and at the end of the plot, because there are almost no pixels that have very high or very low values. The `tuberculosis_sample` image, on the other side, has most of its pixels with dark values, corresponding to the background or the big rounded area with dark gray intensities. Consequently, its histogram has two modes on the left of the plot (where the dark pixels are represented), and since the bright pixels are so few, the right of the histogram is almost empty.

When we want to plot the histogram of a stack, ImageJ will ask if we want to include all the slices in the histogram calculation. In that case, all voxels (all pixels in all the slices of the stack) will be used to plot the histogram. But we may want to evaluate how the intensity is distributed in every slice. For that purpose, you can use the **Live** button that you will find in the Histogram plot. When it is activated, the histogram will correspond only to the current slice, and will be dynamically updated when you change it. Test this feature on sample image `T1 head`. Open the image, display the histogram (**Analyze | Histogram** (*H*)), and click on **Yes** when asked to include all the 129 images. The plotted histogram is calculated from the whole stack. Now, click on the **Live** button and see how the histogram is updated when you change the slice in the stack.

Image histograms are used to explore the intensity distribution in the image in order to transform the intensity values. We could select which intensity range we want to display in the screen, and all values outside of the range will be represented with the minimum or maximum intensity. The original values are not modified; it is the intensity mapping, which is performed when every original value is assigned a specific gray or color value to display in the screen, that is changed. Open the sample image named `CT` to exemplify this concept. If you plot the histogram, you will see that the original image has values from -719 to 1402. This 2121 intensity values must be mapped to 256 gray levels in the computer screen.

While examining the histogram, you will notice that many intensity values have almost no pixel counts. Instead of using gray levels to represent pixels that are almost never present in the image, we could use all our possible 256 gray levels to represent the area of the histogram that has information content.

How do we modify the intensity range from the original image that is displayed in the screen using the 256 gray levels? ImageJ offers several alternatives. Select the window containing the CT image and go to **Image | Adjust | Brightness/Contrast...** (*Ctrl + Shift + C*). Image intensities from -200 to 300 are being mapped to all the 256 gray levels in the screen. All values from -719 (image minimum) to -200 will be black in the image window, and all values from 300 to 1402 (image maximum) will be white. The **B&C** window also shows the histogram so we can check which area is being mapped in the screen. If we modify the minimum and maximum values, the intensity mapping will be updated, and if we click on the **Auto** button, ImageJ will optimize the values in order to allow only a small percentage of the pixels to be saturated (displayed as black or white). The **Brightness** and **Contrast** sliders are a different way of modifying the intensity values displayed; the first one moves the whole range left or right over the histogram, and the latter increases or decreases the range itself:

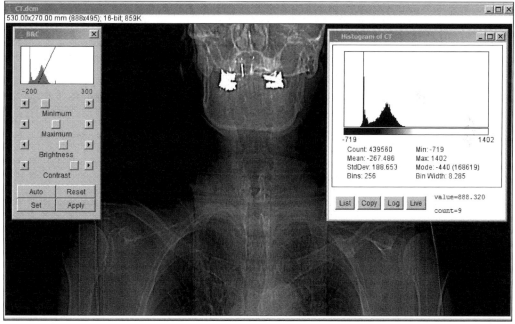

Image sample CT.dcm with histogram and Brightness/Contrast (B&C) windows opened. B&C shows that all pixels below -200 are displayed in black, pixels above 300 will be white, and the range in between are mapped to gray values from 0 to 255 in the image window.

Window and Level (available from **Image | Adjust | Window/Level...**) is a tool similar to the **Brightness** and **Contrast** sliders. The **Level** is the center of the intensity range that is displayed on the screen, and **Window** is the width of that range. For instance, if you click on the **Reset** button in the **Window/Level** window, the **Level** is placed in the center of the histogram, and the **Window** width is the whole image range.

You may have been asking yourself why ImageJ selected the specific range from -200 to 300 when we opened the CT sample image. This range was stored in the image metadata as window width and level values. You can check it by selecting the CT image window and going to **Image | Show Info...** (*I*). A lot of fields are displayed (coming from the original DICOM file), and if you look at the end of the list you will find these values:

- **0028,1050 Window Center: 50**
- **0028,1051 Window Width: 500**

These values correspond to an intensity range centered at 50, that starts at 50 - (500 / 2) and ends at 50 + (500 / 2). Voilà!

Another interesting way to adjust the displayed intensities to the range that maximizes the visualization of an area of the image is by drawing a selection over that area (for instance, using the rectangular selection tool, which is the leftmost button in the toolbar, and then clicking and dragging over the desired area), and then clicking on the **Auto** button in the B&C window. ImageJ will show the histogram of that area and adjust the displayed range. With this method, we can focus our display parameters on different areas:

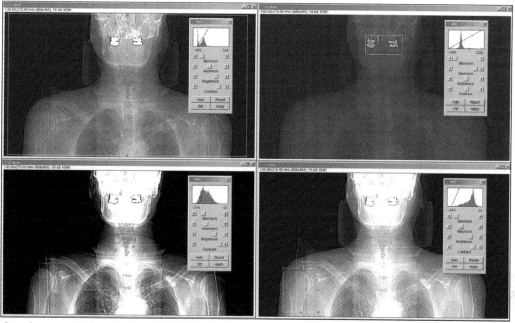

Sample image CT.dcm displayed with four intensity adjustments automatically calculated from four selections (in yellow over every image). The histogram is different for every case because it corresponds to the selection. The selections are whole image (top left), teeth (top right), lung (bottom left), and arm bone (bottom left).

Adjusting brightness and contrast in color images is a process similar to the one described. If you want to modify the Red, Green, and Blue channels independently, use **Image | Adjust | Color Balance...** to select the one you want to adjust.

Thresholding

Until now we have learned what image types ImageJ can handle, how to read these images on how their values are displayed in the computer screen. But at the beginning of this book, we have told you that ImageJ has more to do with quantification than with display, so you may be asking when we will start obtaining some information from our images. In this section, we are going to learn how to segment a digital image using intensity thresholding. **Segmentation** is the process of obtaining which pixels in the image belong to one or several regions of interest. With intensity thresholding, we can do this labeling depending on the intensity value of each pixel. We have learned in the previous section that the histogram plots the intensity distribution in the image, so it is going to be a good tool for intensity thresholding.

Intensity thresholding is simple. We will classify pixels as belonging to a segmented region of interest or not, depending on if their intensity value is inside a certain range. It is difficult to select this range just by taking a look at the image, but if we can interactively modify this range while displaying the resulting segmentation, it is much easier. This can be done using **Image | Adjust | Threshold...** (*Ctrl + Shift + T*). Let's test it on the tuberculosis_sample.tif test image. The threshold interface will automatically select a range (two threshold values) and the resulting segmentation will be the pixels within that range. The default mode to display the result is named **Over/Under**: those pixels with values below the lower threshold are displayed in blue, and the ones above the higher threshold in green. You can change this option to **Red** (segmented pixels in red) or **B&W** (segmented pixels in black, remaining in white, which is the way masks are visualized).

Your selection in the way ImageJ presents thresholding results (**Over/Under**, **Red**, or **B&W**) will be saved in ImageJ.cfg, so that every time you reopen ImageJ, the last used mode will be selected.

There are several methods to calculate the optimal threshold in terms of classification. These methods minimize parameters such as intraclass variance (the variance of the intensity values of the segmented pixels or background pixels). ImageJ has 16 of these automatic threshold calculation methods implemented. Every time you select one of them, threshold values are modified according to that method, and your manual values are lost. When you click on **Apply**, the segmented pixels will be assigned a value of 255, the remaining will be set to 0. You can see the different segmentation display modes in the tuberculosis image. The lower and upper threshold limits are 47 and 80, respectively, so it is segmenting the bright regions of the image, but leaving out the brightest spots. You will need to check the **Dark Background** checkbox in the **Threshold** dialog.

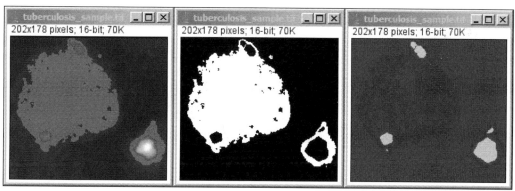

Different visualization modes during the thresholding process: Red (left), B&W (center), and Over/Under (right).

Despite being a 16-bit image, the maximum gray value in `tuberculosis_sample.tif` is 255. This file could have been stored as an 8-bit image, but this allows us to show that the bit depth only defines the maximum and minimum theoretical values a pixel may have, but the actual contents of the image do not need to use all of them and may in fact, be constrained to a small range.

It is not necessary to lose your original image if what you wanted was to make some measurements in the segmented region. Open the tuberculosis image again (in case, you have overwritten it with your thresholding result). Go to **Analyze | Set Measurements....** In this interface, you can select the measures you are interested in (**Area, Min & max gray value, Perimeter...**). If you check the **Limit to threshold** option, these measures will be calculated for the segmented pixels only. Now, repeat the thresholding process, and without closing the threshold interface, perform measures on your region (with **Analyze | Measure** (*Ctrl + M*)). If you repeat this process with different thresholds, you will obtain different measures.

The thresholding process can also be applied to stacks. In that case, you could use the whole stack histogram, or the one corresponding to the current slice. The following snapshot corresponds to the result of Otsu's automatic thresholding on the T1 head stack:

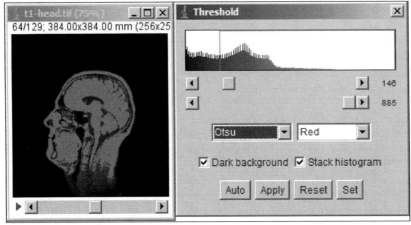

Otsu's automatic threshold on the T1 head stack. Segmented pixels are shown in red.

Image resizing

The zoom options that we explained at the beginning of the chapter allow you to focus on certain regions of the image, but do not modify its contents. However, on some occasions, it may make sense to resize the image, making it actually bigger or smaller. There are two different ways you can accomplish it.

The first one involves resizing the image, and expanding or shrinking the pixel values so that they fit into the new dimensions. This is accomplished by selecting **Image | Adjust | Size...**:

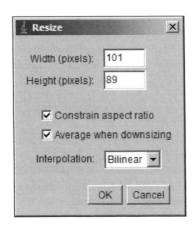

In the dialog that appears, you can select the new image dimensions. If the **Constrain aspect ratio** option is checked, you only need to set the new width, and the height will be automatically filled. If it is bigger than the original image, the contents will be expanded using the selected interpolation.

The other option involves changing the image canvas. This is done using **Image | Adjust | Canvas Size...**:

So, what is the difference between these two methods? With the first one, the contents of the image are accommodated inside the new dimensions. With the second one, the image area is expanded or shrunk, but the image size is the same. If you make the area bigger, the original image will be placed in the selected position, unmodified, and the added voxels will be filled with zero values. If you make the area smaller, the image will be cropped, but not resized. The following image shows the difference between both the methods. We have resized one of the tuberculosis images and have expanded its width to 300 pixels from an original value of 202:

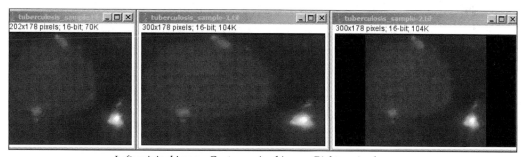

Left: original image. Center: resized image. Right: resized canvas.

Summary

In this chapter, you have seen how to perform basic image operations using ImageJ on a variety of image formats with special emphasis on adjusting different image parameters such as window/level and size. Now that you are familiarized with these simple operations, you are ready to go on to the next chapter, where we will show you how to perform more complex operations, such as local measurements or filtering.

3
Advanced Image Processing with ImageJ

In the previous chapter, we learned how to read images, the types of images that we can handle, and how to manipulate the intensity levels in order to improve visualization or segment part of the pixels depending on their intensity values. Now we will extend our abilities to measure and manipulate our images. First we will learn what are selections, regions of interest, and overlays, and how to work with them and what can be measured using these tools. After this, we will focus on some classic image processing both in spatial and frequency domains, understanding what that means. Finally, we will see how particle analysis can be done in ImageJ.

Selecting regions of your image

This section will deal with the process of selecting different regions in your image (lines or whole areas) so that you can perform local measurements using only those selections. Selections, or regions of interest (ROIs), are the basis of region analysis in ImageJ, and open the door to advance measuring of the information in your image, so let's devote some paragraphs to clarify the initial concepts. Let's start by drawing a few lines.

Basic selections – lines, length, and profiles

Open the `tuberculosis.tif` test image. It is a multichannel image (one 2D image for Red, another for Green, and the last for Blue) and we will use it because working with selections on images of more than two dimensions offers some extra possibilities. The tool to draw a line is the fifth one from the right on the **ImageJ** toolbar with a line icon. When you move the mouse over it, the status bar will indicate the kind of things you can do. You will probably think that there are too many things in the description for a single tool, but you can actually use four different tools from the same button. This is always true in ImageJ for tools showing a small red arrow at the bottom right of the tool button. Right-clicking on the tool shows a menu with the similar available tools.

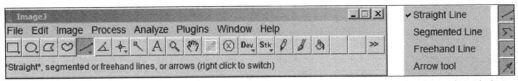

The ImageJ main window with a straight line tool selected (left) and available options for this tools with their corresponding toolbar icons (right).

Select the straight line tool and draw a line by clicking anywhere on the image and moving the mouse without releasing the mouse button until you want to end your line. While the line is being drawn, the status bar shows relevant information: the current coordinates, the angle of your line with respect to the horizontal and the total length, so you can easily create a line of a specific length. But what if you want to measure your line after you drew it carefully on your image? You only need to navigate to **Analyze | Measure** (*Ctrl + M*). By navigating to **Analyze | Set Measurements...** you can select which measurements you want to obtain. These are the ones that will be shown on a floating window called **Results**. Depending on the particular selections done on your ImageJ installation, the parameters shown on your result window will differ from the ones shown here.

A line can also be used to calculate a profile, that is, a plot of the image values along the line. The profile is a simple yet a very useful tool to extract the values along a line that has some meaning in our image. We can use these values to compare the results from different processing algorithms or imaging devices. Draw a straight line on the top-left corner of the `tuberculosis.tif` image. You should obtain something similar to the following screenshot:

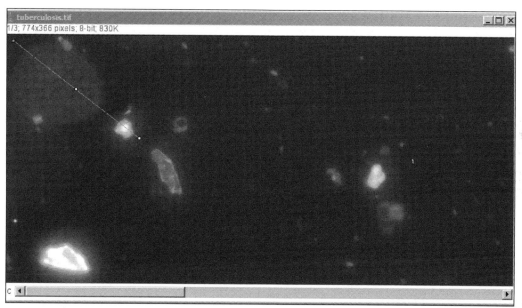

The `tuberculosis.tif` test image with a straight line drawn in order to plot its profile

Now plot the profile by navigating to **Analyze | Plot Profile** (*Ctrl + K*). The resulting profile corresponds to the red channel, the one that was selected on the image with the channel slider at the bottom. Let's check the profile for the different channels by clicking on the **Live** button at the bottom right part of the profile window. Now every time you modify something that influences the profile plotting, the plot will be updated in real time; this also applies to modifications of the line itself by clicking and dragging on the points placed along its length (the mouse pointer changes to a hand to indicate that you can click and modify the line).

Change the channel using the slider at the bottom of `tuberculosis.tif` window, and you will obtain the following profiles:

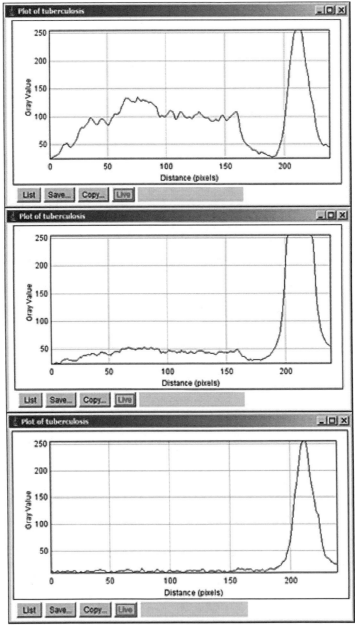

Profiles for the three channels in the `tuberculosis.tif` image, corresponding to Red (top), Green (middle), and Blue (bottom) channels.

The line we have drawn crosses two round shapes. The profiles show the intensities along this line in every channel. The big red shape represents values near 100 in the Red channel, below 50 in the Green, and almost zero in the Blue. The small green shape has very high values in the three channels because it is very intense, with a wider coverage for the Green channel.

There is a simple tool that is also available called **Angle tool**. As you can imagine, by clicking on three independent points it measures the resulting angle. The value is modified if you move any of the vertices.

Results from any measure or profile can be saved in a text file extensions, allowing you to analyze these data with other software such as Microsoft Excel.

Drawing regions of interest over an area

In the previous section we presented the straight line tool and also indicated that the corresponding button in the toolbar allows selecting another three tools: **Segmented Line**, **Freehand Line**, and **Arrow Tool**. These are a part of a group of tools that ImageJ facilitates in order to draw selections, that are areas of the image that can be used to measure all kinds of parameters (area, length, maximum, perimeter, and so on) or to specify which pixels of the image will be taken into account in further processing steps.

We can draw ROIs by combining several tools. The simplest one is the straight line. All these tools are together in the **ImageJ** toolbar, and are as follows:

- Rectangle and rounded rectangle tools [⬜]
- Oval and elliptical selections, selection brush [⬭]
- Polygon [◁]
- Freehand [◠]
- Straight, segmented, and freehand lines [◢]

Instead of giving a full description of what every tool is and how it is used, we will give you some general guidelines that apply to all of them. After reading them, we will propose you play with them for a while so that you can practice.

All tools (except the selection brush) create a shape by clicking with the mouse and moving it without releasing the button until you want to finish. If the tool has options, they can be accessed by double-clicking on the tool icon. The polygon tool creates a side of your polygon every time you click, and closes the shape by double-clicking.

When you have created your selection, it can be translated by clicking on it and moving the mouse before releasing the button, provided that the mouse cursor is showing an arrow icon ( ). The ROI can be modified by clicking and moving any of the control points, and in that case the mouse icon will change to a small hand ( ). When this resizing is done, while holding down a modifier key some restrictions are applied: *Shift* forces a 1:1 aspect ratio of the selection, *Ctrl* forces resizing from the center of the selection, and *Alt* keeps the original aspect ratio. These keys have different effects depending on the kind of selection, and in some cases they won't have any effect. Arrow keys also move the selection, and when combined with *Alt*, they resize the selection pixel by pixel. Draw different ROIs on any sample image and try all this with different selection tools to understand the possibilities better.

When creating selections to be combined with existing ones, use the *Shift* and *Alt* keys as modifiers to add and delete newly created selections to existing ones. If you have a selection in your image and want to combine it with the one you are going to create, press *Shift* while creating it. On the other side, press *Alt* while creating a selection and it will be removed from the existing one. The result is called a composite selection.

Finally, the polygon selection has control points that can be moved independently. If after drawing your polygon you would like to have more control points than the ones you have created, you can click on one control point and press *Shift* at the same time. The existing control point splits into two, allowing a more detailed modification of the selection. If you prefer to remove some control point just click on it and press the *Alt* key. An ROI created with the freehand tool won't have control points, but ImageJ offers a way to convert it into a smooth curve with control points by navigating to **Edit | Selection | Fit Spline**.

As a final exercise, try to obtain the following ROIs on the `tuberculosis_sample.tif` image as follows:

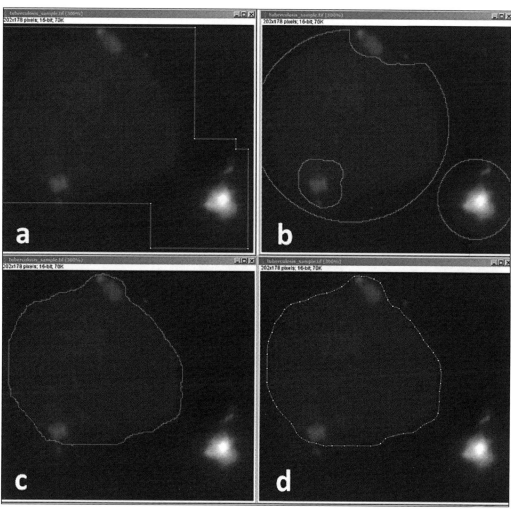

Four examples of ROIs drawn on the tuberculosis_sample.tif image using rectangular selections (a), circular selections (b), freehand selections (c), and this last example converted to a spline curve (d).

Now that you have full control of how to draw different kinds of selections, check how a profile plot can be drawn also from a polyline or a freehand line.

The remaining type of tool is the wand tool [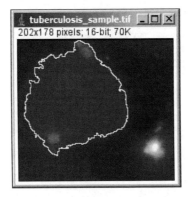]. This tool is a bit different from the previous ones, as it does not require you to draw the desired contour, but instead generates one based on the pixel values of the region surrounding the initial click. This is called region growing segmentation. When you double-click on the tool icon, a dialog will be shown asking for **Mode** and the **Tolerance**. The tolerance is the amount of change that will be permitted in the pixels included in the region, compared to the value of the pixel used as a seed (the one that is being clicked on). The mode selection can be used to impose additional restrictions, such as the need for the pixels to be connected with other pixels already in the region.

The following example shows the application of this tool on the `tuberculosis_sample.tif` image using the Legacy mode and a tolerance of 20.0. You can see that it automatically draws your contour around pixels with values within the range defined by the tolerance:

If you want to remove any selections in the image, the easiest way is to select the rectangular region tool and click (but not drag) on any point outside the current selection. When you click on an image with an area selection tool, existing ROIs are deleted. It may sometimes happen that you have accidentally created a very small region and your analysis results are not the ones you are expecting, so this is a very fast way of removing this possible source of errors.

Finally, you can also set regions consisting of an individual pixel using a single point (or multipoint) tool [⊹].

The ROI manager and the image overlay

In the previous section, you have probably observed that it is very easy to lose your ROI by clicking outside of it. Although we have been working always with a single selection, it does not seem very useful to draw a ROI every time we want to analyze it. ImageJ offers a very powerful tool for this called the ROI manager. It will help you in organizing the ROIs, and also to analyze them.

Open the `tuberculosis.tif` image. Now navigate to **Analyze | Tools | ROI Manager...** Display only the Red channel by navigating to **Image | Color | Channels Tool...** (*Ctrl + Shift + Z*). Every time you draw a selection you can add it to the ROI manager by clicking on the **Add** (t) button. This way you can create several independent ROIs that can be updated whenever necessary. After adding the region in the ROI manager you may rename it or modify its properties (for instance, the color). The default name used in the ROI manager is a combination of the ROI coordinates. You can also select a single region to be active by clicking on its name in the ROI list, and even several of them by clicking with the *Shift* or *Ctrl* keys pressed. Try to obtain the following result on `tuberculosis.tif`:

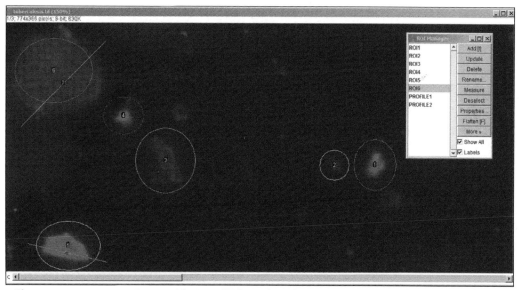

The `tuberculosis.tif` image with six oval ROIs and two line selections added to the ROI manager, each with a different color. Note that in order to see all the ROIs in the ROI manager at the same time, the **Show all** checkbox must be checked.

Drawing ROIs over an image usually has one goal: measuring parameters on those ROIs. **ROI Manager** also facilitates this step. If we select the first six ROIs in the previous example (by clicking on **ROI1** and then on **ROI6** while pressing down the *Shift* key) and then clicking on the **Measure** button, the following window pops up:

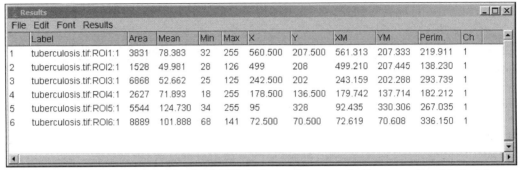

The Results window after measuring the six ROIs in the previous example. You can easily relate the Mean column with the average ROI intensity in the image.

These results are related to the Red channel that we have selected in this multichannel image (notice the last column in the **Results** window called Ch). But if we want to measure all channels (or slices in 3D images) and all ROIs at the same time, we can also do it by navigating to **More | Multi Measure** in the **ROI Manager** window. The result will have one row per channel, and multiple columns corresponding to different ROIs. Profiles can also be compared by navigating to **More | Multi Plot**. Use these tools after selecting the two last ROIs called PROFILE1 and PROFILE2 in our example.

Remember that the **Measure results** window shown in our examples may be different from the ones that you obtain, because the parameters that will be measured are specified by navigating to **Analyze | Set Measurements....**

After all that we have learned, you won't assume that you have to lose your work when closing ImageJ. There are two ways to store ROIs: from the ROI Manager or using the Image Overlay. The ROI Manager stores single ROIs by navigating to **More | Save...** in files with the `.roi` extension, and multiple ROIs in `.zip` files. You will need to select the ROIs that you want to save. In a future ImageJ session you can easily recover them from the ROI Manager (**More | Open...**).

The Image Overlay is like an invisible ROI Manager. It stores the selections or ROIs until you call them back. It is not easy to interact with the ROIs in the Image Overlay, but it has an advantage of being stored with the image when using the TIFF file format. The best way to store your ROIs in the Overlay is to select them and add them to the Overlay by navigating to **Image | Overlay | From ROI Manager**. After saving your image in the TIFF format, you will be able to recover your ROIs while opening the file by navigating to **Image | Overlay | To ROI Manager** (the ROI names will probably experience some modifications).

Filters

First of all, remember, a digital image is a matrix in which each cell contains a different value, a number or group of numbers (think RGB images, which contains a triplet). That number defines an intensity within a certain scale (8 bit, 16 bit, 32 bit images) and certain conventions (black is 0, white is the maximum value). When you change the value of a pixel, it reflects in a change in the grayscale or color representation on the screen. Filters are mathematical functions that generate new pixel values from old ones. There are many applications to this, from noise removal to edge detection.

Image filtering in the spatial domain

The process of assigning new pixel values depending on the values of each pixel and its neighbors is called filtering in the spatial domain, and is achieved through a mathematical operation called convolution. In our context, it consists of taking the original image and a second, smaller one, called kernel or mask. The values in the mask are called weights. The convolution operation takes every pixel in the original image, places the mask on top of it with the mask center on the pixel whose value we wish to change, and calculates the new pixel value as the weighted sum of the original one and its neighbors.

The weights for every pixel are the values of the mask. The process is depicted in the following diagram:

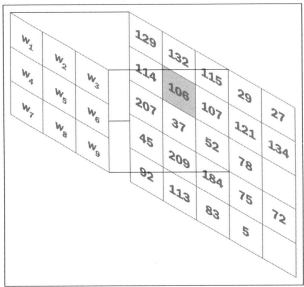

Original image to be processed (right) and convolution mask (left) that contains the weights to be applied to every surrounding pixel.

The original image is shown to the right. If we want to calculate the new value for the shaded pixel, that has current value 106, we will need to apply the following formula:

$$\text{new pixel value} = w_1 . 129 + w_2 . 132 + w_3 . 115 + w_4 . 114 + ... + w_9 . 52$$

This process has to be applied to every pixel in the image. Without specifying the values of the weights, you would probably not understand the purpose of this process. But let's suppose that all weights (w1, w2, ..., w9) are equal to $\frac{1}{9}$. In that case, for every pixel the new value is the average of the original pixel and its eight neighbors. Depending on the values that we introduce in the mask, a different process will be applied to the original image.

You can notice that there may be a problem when computing the new value of a pixel placed on the image edge, as part of the kernel falls outside the limits of the image. In those cases, several solutions can be applied: either we imagine that the outside of the image is composed of black pixels (value = 0) or we artificially duplicate the edge pixel values, so that the mask has some value under its weights. ImageJ uses this second solution internally, so you do not need to worry about it.

Let's work a little on the meaning of a mask that has all weights equal to $\frac{1}{9}$. This filtering is called smoothing: when the original pixel has an intensity value similar to its neighbors, the resulting value will not be very different to the original. But those pixels with values very different from their neighbors will be substituted by a value more similar to their neighborhood. Overall, the image will look blurred. Although this blurring may not seem interesting, it will remove noise, converting noisy areas in the image into homogeneous ones. As a side effect, it will also smooth the edges.

The larger the mask, the greater will be the number of neighboring pixels that will be included in the convolution. All the weight values need not be the same. If we want to give more weight to central pixels and less to the surrounding ones, we will be calculating a weighted average, and consequently the image will be smoothed but with less degradation of the edges than when using the standard average.

There are several ways to apply smoothing filters in ImageJ, which are as follows:

- Navigating to **Process | Smooth** applies a smooth average with 3 x 3 mask size.

- Navigating to **Process | Filters | Convolve...** shows an interface that allows creating your own odd-sized mask specifying the weights. For instance, three rows with values 1, 1, and 1 is equivalent to a smooth average with 3 x 3 mask size.

- Navigating to **Process | Filters | Mean...** lets you specify the radius of the mask, and also has a **Preview** checkbox.

- One common weighted average is available by navigating to **Process | Filters | Gaussian Blur...** In this case, a gaussian function centered in the current pixel is used to calculate the weights. You will be asked to provide the standard deviation (sigma) of this gaussian function. Higher values will result in more smoothing. The sigma value is by default in pixels, although you have a checkbox to indicate if you want to use scaled image units.

Let's put all concepts together in the following exercise. Open the `CT_rat_head.tif` test image four times (navigate to **File | Open** four times to obtain four equivalent windows or open it once and navigate to **Image | Duplicate...** (*Ctrl + Shift + D*) to make three copies). The first one will be kept unchanged. Process the second with a mean filter with radius 1.5 pixels, and the third with a mean filter with radius 3.0 pixels (available by navigating to **Process | Filters | Mean...**). Finally, apply a gaussian blur with sigma = 1.0 to the last one (**Process | Filters | Gaussian Blur...**). The last step is to measure the difference between the filters. For this, we need to draw an oval selection which is exactly the same on the center of the images. Draw the selection on one of the images, select the window of the next one, and navigate to **Edit | Selection | Restore Selection** (*Ctrl + Shift + E*) to create the same selection.

Finally, we want to measure the standard deviation of the intensity values inside the selection for every image (original and processed). Make sure that standard deviation is one of the parameters you will measure (by navigating to **Analyze | Set Measurements...**). Now navigate to **Analyze | Measure** (*Ctrl + M*) after selecting every image. The **Results** window should look similar to the following screenshot:

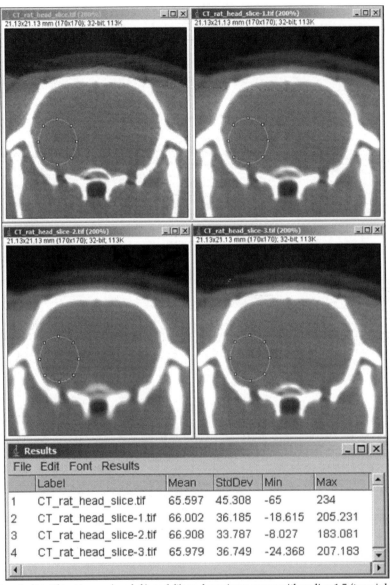

The CT_rat_head_slice.tif test image (top left) and filtered versions: mean with radius 1.5 (top right), mean with radius 3.0 (middle left) and gaussian blur with sigma 1.0 (middle right). The Results window at the bottom corresponds to the measures in the green selection.

What we can learn from these results is that all smoothing filters decrease the standard deviation in the measured selection, because that area is more homogeneous after filtering. For the mean filter, larger radius corresponds to larger filter and consequently lower standard deviation (more noise removed), but also more blurring of the edges. Finally, with the gaussian blur we obtain a similar standard deviation than with mean with radius 1.5, but with slightly more edge preservation.

The last filter that may be very useful for certain kinds of noise is the median filter. In this case, instead of applying the mask to the image with convolution, the original pixel value is substituted by the median value of the pixels under the mask. This is a non-linear process (while convolution is linear) that has two main advantages:

- Median filter removes pixels that have much higher or much lower value than its neighbors (what is usually called the salt and pepper noise)

- Median filter preserves edges, because it does not introduce new values in the image (as the mean filter does)

Open the `CT_rat_head_Salt_and_Pepper.tif` test image. We have to recognize that this image is really noisy. Now apply a median filter with radius 1.0 by navigating to **Process | Filter | Median...**. You will be surprised with the following result:

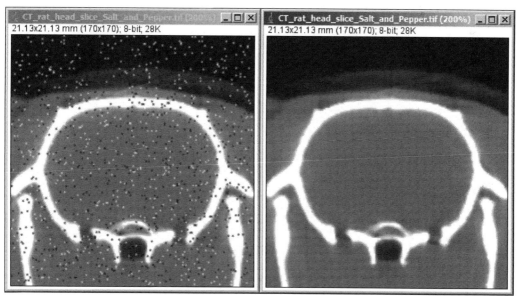

Image with salt and pepper noise (left) and the result of a median filter with radius 1.0 (right).

The spatial filters that we have discussed can also be applied to stacks in 3D. This means that the mask has three dimensions, and consequently not only the pixels in X and Y directions are averaged (for the mean filter), but they are also averaged in the Z direction. You can find them by navigating to **Process | Filters** with a prefix 3D in their names.

By navigating to the **Process | Noise | Remove Outliers...** menu option, the median filter of the specified radius is applied when the pixel under the mask deviates from the surrounding ones more than a configurable threshold.

Edge detection

One particularly useful application of spatial filtering is edge detection. An edge in a grayscale image is a discontinuity that separates two regions. There are several ways we can detect edges, the most immediate of them being a filter in the spatial domain.

Consider the next image (the vborder.tif test image):

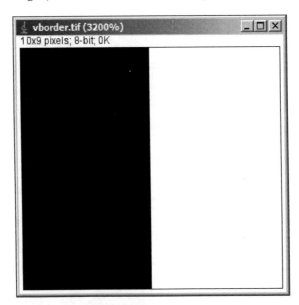

As you can see in the information line located on top of the image, this is a very small matrix (10 x 9, note the zoom level!), but it is enough for us to comment on simple edge detection methods. The image has only two different pixel values: 0 on the left side (black) and 255 on the right side (white). The border in this image is exactly in the middle of the image, dividing the black from the white region.

The most direct way to detect a border of this kind is to use a simple convolution kernel. Consider the following case, written in the format you would use when running the **Process | Filter | Convolve...** tool:

-1 0 1

-2 0 2

-1 0 1

This is called the (vertical) Sobel operator. You have already seen how spatial filtering works: the original image is convolved with this matrix and the resulting pixel values are used to form a new image with the filtered values. Now think about what this matrix does as it moves over the preceding screenshot:

- When the whole matrix is over a homogeneous area, the resulting value is zero. You can check that this is true, independently of the value of the pixels under the kernel.

- When there is a difference in the values on the right-most column (or the rightmost column and central column; suppose the kernel moves from left to right), the value is nonzero. When the mask passes completely to the other side, it is zero again.

You can test this yourself by navigating to **Process | Filters | Convolve...** and writing the preceding matrix. You should get a result similar to the following one:

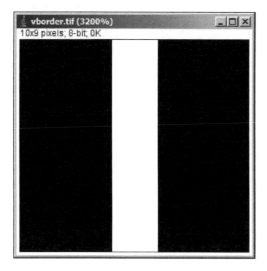

As you can see, the vertical edge in the original image has been detected by the filter. There is an equivalent horizontal Sobel operator, which is like the previous one but rotated 90°. That filter can be used to detect horizontal edges. By navigating to the **Process | Find Edges** menu option we can run both the operators which returns the square root of the squared results:

$$E = \sqrt{S_x^2 + S_y^2}$$

This operation finds all the edges in the image. You can try running that command on the CT_slice_test.dcm test image; this image is much more complex than the simple one we have used to explain how these filters work, but the underlying mechanism remains exactly the same. The following screenshot shows both the original image on the left and the edges detected by the **Find Edges** option on the right. Note that all the edges have been found. As an exercise, try convolving the original image only with the horizontal or vertical kernels, and see what result you obtain:

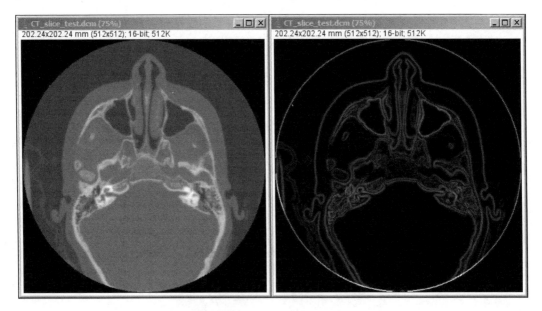

Probably, when you applied the **Find Edges** operation, the resulting image was completely black. This is due to the window/level settings of the image, so you will have to adjust the contrast (by navigating to **Image | Adjust | Brightness/Contrast...**(*Ctrl + Shift + C*) and by clicking on **Auto**). This is something quite common, so always take a look at this before concluding that your analysis erases the original image if you encounter this at some point.

There are other operators that you might want to try:

- The Prewitt kernel is very similar to the Sobel one, but does not weigh more heavily on the center row/column.

  -1 0 1   1 1 1

  -1 0 1   0 0 0

  -1 0 1   -1 -1 -1

These two kernels are, in effect, differential operators: they compute the first order derivative of the image in the axis they are applied to. There is a kernel that computes the second order derivative, and that is the Laplacian operator. It detects more subtle borders, but precisely because of that, it is much more sensitive to noise. There are several different formulations, depending on whether they include the diagonals or not and where the sign is included:

0 1 0	0 -1 0	1 1 1	-1 -1 -1
1 -4 1	-1 4 -1	1 -8 1	-1 8 -1
0 1 0	0 -1 0	1 1 1	-1 -1 -1

In the following screenshot, you can see several different applications of these kernels on the CT image shown previously. The window/level settings have been set to exactly the same values (from -32741 to -32684) for all images, so you can see the difference in effects:

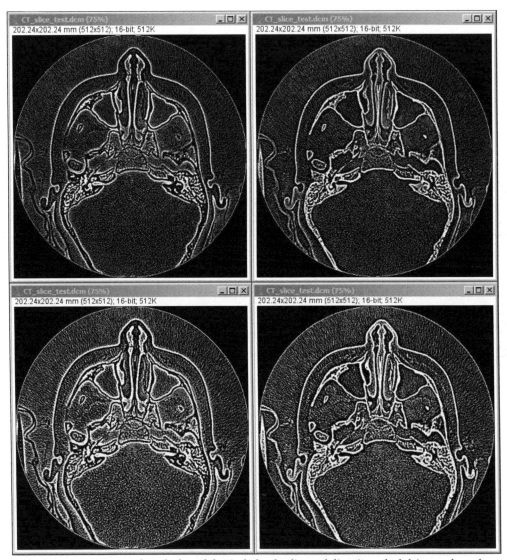

The lower row corresponds to the kernel that includes the diagonal directions; the left images have the center pixel with the negative value.

All the different spatial filters that we have presented (smoothing, median, edge detection, and so on) can be applied only to a certain region of the image. Draw a selection before running the filtering process, and the only pixels affected will be those inside the selection.

The Fourier transform

The Fourier transform, named after *Jean Baptiste Joseph Fourier* (1768-1830), is a mathematical operation that gives us another way to represent our image. Instead of using the spatial coordinates as arguments in our image, in the Fourier space, the argument is frequency. Every position corresponds to the weight that a certain frequency has in our image. The algorithm that ImageJ (and many other programs) uses to convert our image to the frequency space is called **FFT (Fast Fourier Transform)**.

You are probably wondering what the entire previous paragraph meant. As we have done several times before, let's explain it with an example. Open the sin_pattern_1.tif and sin_pattern_2.tif images:

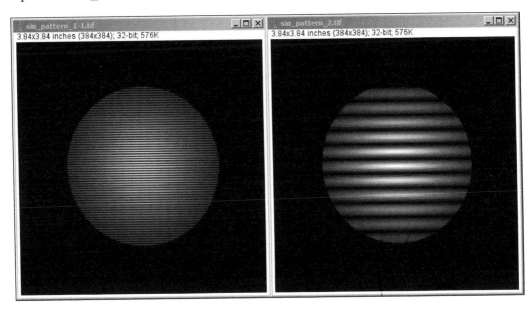

Both images represent a sinusoidal pattern of intensity levels that change when we move in the vertical direction over the image. Let's calculate now the Fourier transform value of each image by navigating to **Process | FFT | FFT**:

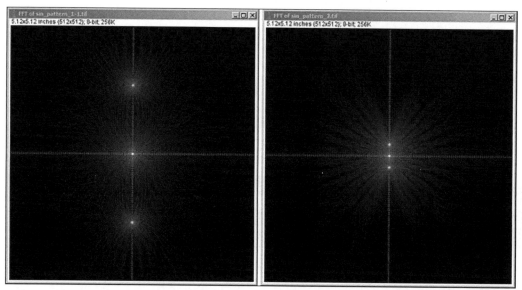

The result of calculating FFT for the `sin_pattern_1.tif` (left) and `sin_pattern_2.tif` (right) images. The window and level settings have been adjusted to improve visualization.

The bright spots in the FFT represent frequencies that are present in the image. For the first image, the sinusoidal pattern varies more rapidly than in the second, which means higher frequency. The zero frequency (the origin) is in the center of Fourier space, and more distance from the center means higher frequency. Fourier transform has some symmetries (the explanations for this are beyond the scope of this book), so the bright spots appear always in pairs with respect to the origin. What you have to understand is that in Fourier space: the positions near the center are of low frequencies, and longer distances from this origin represent higher frequency.

What happens if we rotate the original image? In our example, the bright spots in the FFT appeared in the vertical axis, because the sinusoidal intensity pattern had vertical direction. If it was in the horizontal direction, the FFT would also have rotated. Apart from these basic images, we can also calculate the FFT of real images, as we will see in the next section.

Image filtering in the frequency domain

Not only can the FFT of any image can be obtained, but also the inverse operation. In the previous examples, if you select the FFT of one image and navigate to **Process | FFT | Inverse FFT** you will recover the original image. But what if we modify the FFT before coming back to the spatial domain? In this section we will learn some applications of this process.

Repeat the previous steps (navigating to **File | Open...** and navigating to **Process | FFT | FFT**) with `sinc_pattern_1.tif`. Now we will remove the two bright spots far from the center, which correspond to the sinusoidal pattern. In order to do this, draw two circular selections (press SHIFT to add the second one) over the areas we want to remove. We want to fill those two areas with zero value. First, we need to select a color to be used to fill by navigating to **Image | Color | Color Picker...** (*Ctrl + Shift + K*) and selecting the black color (red = 0, green = 0, blue = 0). Finally, navigate to **Edit | Fill** (*Ctrl + F*) to fill the selection with zero value. Now, calculate the inverse FFT (by navigating to **Process | FFT | Inverse FFT**). Your original image, FFT and its inverse should look as follows:

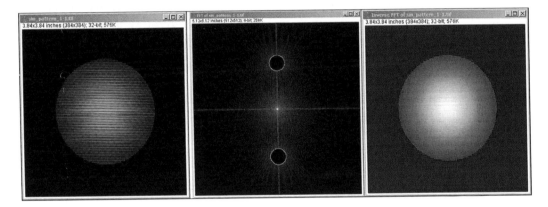

In our result (the right-most image in the screenshot), the high sinusoidal pattern has disappeared, because we have removed that frequency from the FFT and only the frequency components with lower frequency remain.

Another application may be the removal of sinusoidal patterns on an image that is a result of some interference. The following screenshot shows the `MR_interf.tif` test image to the left, and its FFT in the middle:

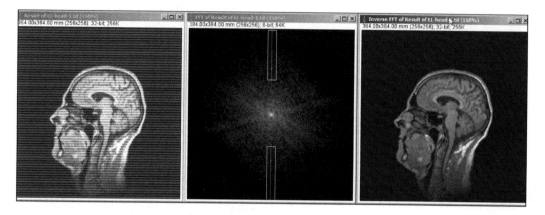

In order to remove the interference, draw the green selection on the FFT as it is shown in the screenshot (use a rectangular selection, and then remove the center pressing the *Alt* key while you draw another rectangle surrounding the center of the FFT). When you calculate the inverse FFT, you will obtain the right-most image in the previous screenshot. As you can see, the artifact has been completely removed without degrading the details in the image.

We have learned what the FFT of an image is, and that if we manipulate the Fourier space the whole image is processed. This has been only an introduction to the possibilities that the frequency domain offers to image processing, but with these concepts you have the basics for further analysis.

Particle analysis

A potentially useful task in many imaging fields, especially in microscopy, is the automatic detection and measurement of the particles present in a given image. Consider the following one, taken from the original set of tuberculosis images that we have presented previously (`tuberculosis_full.tif`):

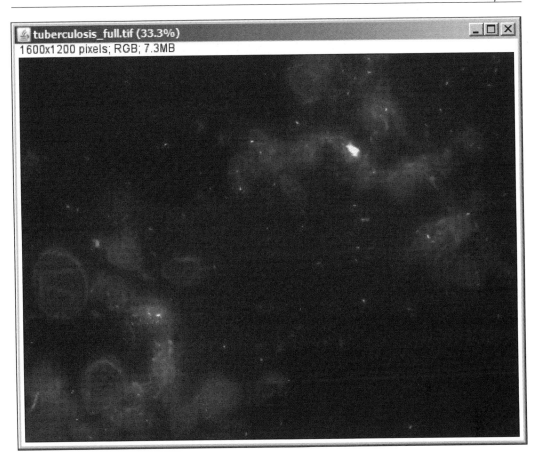

tuberculosis_full.tif (33.3%)
1600x1200 pixels; RGB; 7.3MB

Note that the zoom level has been reduced to show the whole image on the page. If you open that image on ImageJ, you can see that there are many small green objects: those are the Mycobacterium tuberculosis bacilli, and we want to count them. How many of them are there in the image? One way of accomplishing that task is to count them manually. That can be hard even for a single image, and think about having to count hundreds of them. So, let's see if we can get ImageJ to do the job for us.

In the first place, note that this is an RGB color image. When we run the cursor over the image, a triplet of values is shown on the status bar on the main window (one for each Red, Green, and Blue values, with 8 bit to encode each one). As the bacilli are very bright in the green dimension, it would be good to analyze only that channel. We can do this in the following two ways:

- Navigating to **Image | Color | Split channels** takes the original color image and creates three new grayscale images, each one with the intensity value corresponding to each color in the original one

- Navigating to the **Image | Type | RGB** stack accomplishes the same but creates a single stack with three slices, one for each color

We will be using the second method in this exercise, but you can try replicating what we did with the first one. If you try it and move through the slices, you can see how the different colors are codified. The bacilli are much brighter in the second slice, which, as is to be expected, belongs to the intensity of the green color.

We now stick to this slice and remove the image background. That is done by navigating to the **Process | Subtract Background...** menu option. We have selected the following parameters:

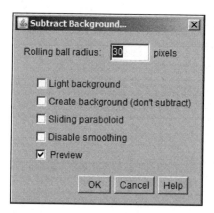

What this command does is that it removes all the background elements and sets the background pixels to a value as close to 0 as possible, while leaving intact the brightest particles. When we click on **OK**, the following dialog will show up:

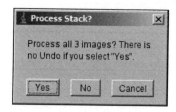

It is common for many ImageJ commands to ask the user whether the selected operation must be applied to the whole stack or only to the active slice. In this case, we do not really want to apply the operation to the red and blue slices, so we click on **No**. If we click on **Yes**, the operation will take a bit longer, but there will be no difference in the final result.

So now we have the green intensity of the image clear, without the background elements that might mislead us. Now we need to threshold the image to use the automatic particle analyzer. We have chosen the "Moments" automatic method by navigating to **Image | Adjust | Threshold** (*Ctrl + Shift + T*), as it yields a very good result for this particular case. Do not use the **Stack histogram** option, as we want to use only the green color's information for thresholding. We close the image (check that the threshold has been applied) and then navigate to **Analyze | Analyze Particles** with the following options:

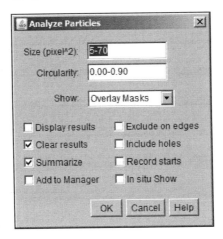

This tool will automatically count all the elements in the image that have a size and shape within the given range. The **Size (pixel^2)** label allows the user to introduce a range of pixel areas in the form (minimum-maximum, and maximum can be infinity). The **Circularity** label asks for the shape of the object, with 0.0 being a line, and 1.0 a circle. We have made preliminary measurements using the wand tool on different bacilli and we have seen that those ranges are appropriate for detecting most of them.

After clicking on **OK**, you will get the following screenshot:

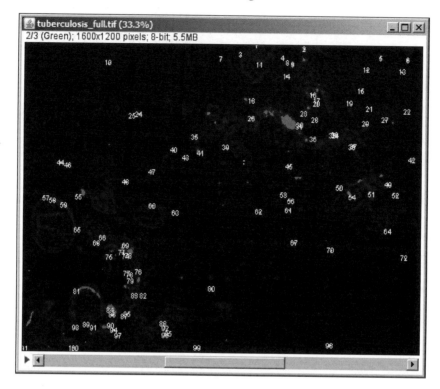

You can see the thresholded slice (using the Red scheme), and every detected particle has been added as an enumerated overlay. Also, you will have a **Results** window that displays the measured parameters as follows:

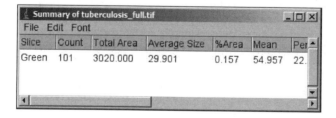

So, how many particles are there in the image? Answer: 101 (more or less, considering the bacilli that are not detected by our method and some false positives for particles that are detected but should not, that are inevitable with any automatic method).

As you can see, this analysis, though faster than the manual method, took us a while. However, ImageJ offers some tools that allow more task automation. Let's advance to the next chapter for some macro programming (even if you are not a programmer).

Summary

In this chapter you have learned how to draw regions of interest over your image, save them for later use, and perform local analysis. Also, the filtering concept has been introduced along with several useful applications. Finally, we have shown how to combine several tools in order to clean an image and perform a particle analysis over it.

So far, we have been doing everything manually. In the next chapter, we will introduce the ImageJ macro system, which will allow you to repeat exactly the same operations on a greater number of images, or to save exactly the processing steps you carry out to ensure repeatability of your measurements.

4
ImageJ Macros

In the previous chapters, you have learned the basics of image processing with ImageJ along with some more advanced techniques. This chapter explains:

- How to use the macro recorder to store analysis steps so that they can be replicated
- How to apply macros to a large number of images
- How to extend your knowledge beyond what the recorder offers using some macro language syntax
- A list of common operations that you will encounter during macro development
- How to install macros to access them easily from the main ImageJ menu

What is an ImageJ macro

An ImageJ macro is a small program that contains the sequence of operations performed on an image. This program can then be stored on a disk and rerun at any given time. This will allow you to store the analysis procedures for reproducibility purposes or automatically process many images in exactly the same way.

The macro recorder

The great thing about ImageJ macros is that you don't need any prior programming experience to code them. We will also be doing some programming in any case, but the important thing to note here is that non-technical users can create their own macros effortlessly.

Remember the example that ended the previous chapter and helped us in understanding how the particle analyzer is used. Imagine that you do the analysis, store the results, and forget about it. Six months from now we need to go back to the original data and repeat the analysis (for instance, because some journal reviewers asked us to change some parameter or recheck the original procedure). Chances are that we will get an approximate result, but not the exact one, as there are several parameters that need to be set and you might not remember them. Also, suppose you need to analyze not one but hundreds of images. The semi-automatic method we used is good enough for a few images, but it is still very slow for analyzing many of them. The ImageJ macro system can help us to replicate a large number of operations in a very easy way.

The easiest way of creating a new ImageJ macro is by simply recording all the steps a given analysis requires. Think of an operation in the ImageJ menu option as a command that is executed with the appropriate parameters. All these commands can be recorded and rerun again when needed.

Now we are going to repeat the analysis of the previous chapter but recording what we do. The first thing we need to do is start the macro recorder. This is done by navigating to the **Plugins | Macros | Record...** menu option. An empty recorder window will appear as shown in the following screenshot:

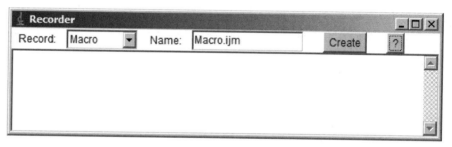

This window will do nothing by itself. You can see that it is possible to type inside the textbox, but nothing happens. The purpose of the macro recorder is to keep track of every command run from the ImageJ menu options (or the equivalent shortcuts). Indeed, we can see that different commands are added to this window as we use different menu options. This is what we should have in this window after performing the analysis (this time, we used the **Image | Color | Split channels** option, so the first operation gives us three images and not a single stack with three slices):

```
run("Split Channels");
selectWindow("tuberculosis_full.tif (blue)");
close();
selectWindow("tuberculosis_full.tif (red)");
close();
```

```
selectWindow("tuberculosis_full.tif (green)");
run("Subtract Background...", "rolling=30");
setAutoThreshold("Moments dark");
run("Analyze Particles...", "size=5-70 circularity=0.00-0.90
show=[Overlay Masks] clear summarize");
```

Downloading the example code

You can download the example code files for all Packt books you have purchased from your account at http://www.packtpub.com. If you purchased this book elsewhere, you can visit http://www.packtpub.com/support and register to have the files e-mailed directly to you.

We accomplished two things: we have run the desired analysis and at the same time we recorded everything we did. See that every action we took generated a command on the recorder. The command not only runs a given tool on the image but also keeps track of the particular parameters that were used at that time. We encourage you to run other commands on the image to see what the recorder does. There are a few commands that do not have an equivalent command line (for example, the **Freehand selections** tool, it will emit a line when it is selected, but will not record the actual contour being drawn). Feel free to explore all the options you can think about, from opening a file to filtering it, duplicating, renaming, resizing, converting its type, and so on.

Now you can save the macro with all the recorded commands. There are two ways of doing that, which are as follows:

- From the recorder window, click on the **Create** button. A new window will appear with the contents of the recorder in it.
- Navigate to **Plugins | New | Macro** from the main ImageJ window and copy and paste all or part of the contents of the recorder window. This option is useful when many commands have been run as a test and we only want to keep a few of them.

No matter what option you choose, you will end up with a text window that contains the commands just recorded. You can now save this file as an ImageJ macro to be run whenever you want.

If you create your macro by clicking on the **Create** button, ImageJ will suggest that you name the file as Macro.ijm (after ImageJMacro). Another method will suggest the name as Macro.txt. The file extension is irrelevant, you can select the full filename when you save it and use whatever extension you like, though .ijm is a bit more descriptive about the file contents and purpose.

It is a good coding practice to comment the code in order to understand what the macro is supposed to do, what input it should accept or any kind of information that may be useful to anyone running it. Comments start with a double slash, //. You can write whatever you want after those symbols and that will be ignored when the macro is run. If you need a comment that spans several lines, use // at the beginning of each one. Comments are only a human-readable explanation about what the code does when you open it after several months from now. So, use them to explain whatever you think a user may need to know when using your macro.

Running macros

So, now we have recorded every step needed for the analysis and stored in it a text file. What if we want to run it again? This is done by navigating to the **Plugins | Macros | Run...** menu option. A file chooser dialog will pop up and we will have to select the file that contains the commands we want to execute. With the tuberculosis image open, choose that menu option, and then the text file we just saved. All the commands will be run one by one and we will end up with exactly the same result as before. Try running the macro for the `tuberculosis_full.tif` measurements and see if you get the same result we got at the end of the previous chapter. In our tests, it takes about two seconds to compute all the calculations! Now you can compare that to the manual way and grasp the power of ImageJ for image processing.

It is also possible to run a macro while we are writing it. This is normally done during the coding process, so we can be sure that it does what it is supposed to do before saving it definitely. From the macro editing window (not the recorder), we can navigate to the **Macros | Run Macro** (*Ctrl + R*) menu option to run all of the commands (or the lines currently selected), or navigate to **Macros | Evaluate Line** (*Ctrl + Y*) to execute only the line under the cursor. This is also useful for trying the different code examples that we will present throughout this chapter. Just create a new macro and copy and paste or type the code and run it from the window.

Modifying a recorded macro

You can open an existing macro file by navigating to **Plugins | Macros | Edit...** You can then do all the modifications you need (for instance, you can restart the recorder and add more commands if you need them, or comment what you did previously), and save the file again.

Note that the macro commands store the parameters used for each tool. Suppose you want to change some of them (for example, setting a rolling ball radius in the background subtraction tool of 40 instead of 30). In that case, you only need to edit the macro file and substitute:

```
run("Subtract Background...", "rolling=30");
```

By the following code:

```
run("Subtract Background...", "rolling=40");
```

Then you can rerun the macro and see the difference in the results.

More about the macro language – basic syntax and operators

Until now, you have learned how to keep track of the menu options you select in order to create a program that executes all of them in a sequential way.

The ImageJ macro language is much richer than just the options output by the macro recorder. This section explains a bit more about the macro programming language.

Variables

You can define your own variables inside the macro language. A very simple example is as follows:

```
message = "Hello, World!";
print(message);
```

This macro simply causes the message, **Hello, World!** to appear on the ImageJ log window. The `print(message)` command outputs its messages there. In this case, the text is contained in the `message` variable. Variables in ImageJmacros may contain any type of data (numeric, strings, arrays) and they need not be declared, they are created when their values are assigned. Another example is as follows:

```
message1 = "Hello, World!";
message2 = 40 + 2;
print(message1, message2);
print(message1 + "" + message2);
```

As you can see, both the methods print the same message (**Hello, World! 42**), despite the `message2` variable storing a numeric value. It is automatically converted to a string when printed.

> Note that the `message2` variable stores the value $40 + 2$ as **42**. All the common mathematical operations are available in the macro language: addition (+), subtraction (-), multiplication (*), division (/), and modulo (%). Exponentiation is done using the `pow(base, exponent)` function (for example, `pow(2,3) = 8`). With this example, you can also see that in string variables, the + symbol is used to concatenate values.

An array is a special type of variable that stores several values at once. These values can be accessed or modified by addressing their position inside the array using square brackets. Arrays are created using the `newArray(arg)` function, with `arg` being either the dimensions of the array or the actual contents separated by commas. An array may contain different type of values. Edit and run the following example:

```
array1 = newArray(2);
print(array1[0], array1[1]);
array1[0] = 42;
array1[1] = "A string value";
print(array1[0], array1[1]);
```

In this macro, we have created an array variable (`array1`) with only two positions. In the beginning, both positions a have value of 0. We then proceed to assign two values, one numeric and another a string. Array positions are addressed using the variable name and then the position (starting at 0) in square brackets. You can see how many elements a given array contains with the `lengthOf(arg)` function, where `arg` is an array variable. If you try to address a position beyond the current capacity of the array (say, `array1[2]` in the previous example), you will get an error message as shown in the following screenshot:

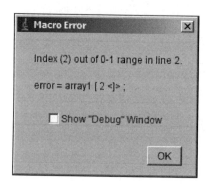

A brief note on debugging a macro

Now that we are at it, in the previous dialog you will have noticed the **Show "Debug" Window** checkbox. If you check it and then click on the **OK** button, the **Debug** window will appear. This window contains all the variables currently stored in your macro file, along with their values or their dimensions, in case of arrays. This is useful when we are trying to find where a coding error may have happened. This window can also be called from the editing window by navigating to the **Debug | Debug Macro** menu option (*Ctrl + D*) of the editing window. Once this window is open, you can use the step-by-step tool to go through each line of your macro to check where the problem lies. When you choose the **Debug Macro** option, the first line of your macro will be highlighted as follows:

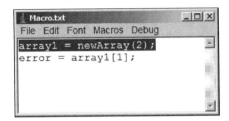

In this debugging mode, navigating to **Debug | Step** (*Ctrl + E*) will execute the highlighted line, and the cursor will move to the next line. By navigating to **Debug | Trace** (*Ctrl + T*), all the lines of code will be executed in a step-by-step fashion.

Control structures

As in any other programming language, the usual control structures (loops, conditionals) are available in the ImageJ macros. The following brief examples show very simple pieces of code to explain their use. You are encouraged to try them on your own and play with them to see how they behave. If you already know some programming, you probably may want to skip this section.

The for loop

The for loop consists of a variable initialization, a continue condition, and an operation that is made after the contents of the loop are executed. Typically, it consists of a counter variable that is incremented until it reaches a certain limit. An example of the for loop is as follows:

```
for(i=0;i<10;i++){
    print("Value of i ="+i);
}
```

The output of the preceding code is as follows:

10 lines of text are displayed starting from **Value of i = 0** to **Value of i = 9**.

The variable i is created inside the loop and has no meaning outside it. The value of the variable has to be less than the specified limit (i<10) and is incremented after each iteration of the loop (i++).

 The i++ construction you have just seen means "increment the value of i in one unit". There is an equivalent to this, i-- that subtracts 1 from the variable's present value. These are "post-increment" and "post-decrement" operators. There also exist the "pre-increment" and "pre-decrement" equivalents (++i, --i). The difference between them is that in post-increment the variable is evaluated and then incremented, and in pre-increment it works the other way round. If i equals 0, print (i++) prints 0, but print (++i) prints 1.

The while loop

The while loop is similar to the for loop, it executes its contents as long as the specified condition is true. An example is as follows:

```
i=0;
while(i<10){
    print("Value of i ="+i);
    i++;
}
```

The output displayed on the screen is exactly the same as in the previous macro.

The if (condition) and if (condition) … else statements

The if statement allows you to perform some operation only if the condition is true. The following macro is similar to the one that was used to explain the for loop, but the printed message depends on the content of the variable, i.

```
for(i = 0; i< 10; i++) {
if (i % 2 == 0) {
    print(i + " is even.");
  } else {
    print(i + " is odd.");
  }
}
```

This little loop identifies which numbers are even and which are odd. The condition checks whether the number modulo 2 is 0. In that case, the number is even. If not (else), the number is odd.

Defining functions

A function is a piece of code that does a very specific operation. Defining functions in the ImageJ macro language is simple. You just need to use the function keyword, followed by the function name. A function may receive as many arguments as desired and may or may not return a value. Consider the following function:

```
functiongetMax(a, b) {
  if (a > b) {
    return a;
  }
  else{
    return b;
  }
}
print(getMax(5, 4));
print(getMax(5, 6));
```

As you can see from the previous example, the function definition does nothing by itself. In order to execute it, it needs to be called.

Some useful procedures

There is a very extensive compilation of all the functions available in the macro language on the ImageJ website (http://rsbweb.nih.gov/ij/developer/macro/functions.html). In this section, we are offering a brief explanation of some of the operations that you are most likely to use. Instead of just listing the name of the necessary functions, we will ask some common questions and then answer them using code.

Note that finding out what command does a specific function is very easy: just start the recorder and run the command you are interested on running in your macro. You can then copy and paste the resulting line and modify the parameters accordingly.

Opening an image from a macro

There are two ways to open an image file from your hard disk (or from a URL).
For an interactive way (you need input from the user, typically the file path) just
run the following line:

```
open();
```

A dialog will appear asking you for the file location inside your hard disk. Just
double click on it and the image will be opened.

The non-interactive way, in which you know in advance the file location,
is very similar:

```
open(path);
```

Here `path` is the location of the file (for example, `C:/temp/image1.jpg`).

It may happen that you want to store the image path into a variable to open it using
a different method (for example, importing a raw image). In that case, we can use the
`File.openDialog(message)` function. It opens a file browser dialog and returns the
path of the selected file. The following code does the same by simply calling `open()`,
but will also store the path in the `mypath` variable using the following code:

```
mypath = File.openDialog("Select a file");
open(mypath);
```

Finding out how many images are open

The number of images currently open in the ImageJ system is stored in a variable
called `nImages`. It updates itself every time a new image is opened. Duplicate images
are count as a just another image. Try the following macro:

```
print(nImages); // No images: 0.
run("Dot Blot (7K)");
print(nImages); // One image: 1.
run("Dot Blot (7K)");
print(nImages); // Two images: 2.
```

As you can see when you run this code, the `run("DotBlot(7K)")` line causes ImageJ
to open the `Dot Blot` sample image.

Obtaining the dimensions of an image

There are several ways of doing that. If you want individual dimensions, you can use the `getHeight()` and `getWidth()` functions. Also, the `nSlices` variable stores the number of slices in the active stack. If you need all the information at once, you can run the `getDimensions(width,height,channels,slices,frames)` function. This function is a bit different from the other functions we have already seen. Instead of returning a value, it sets the `width` variable to the width of the image, the `height` variable to the height of the image, and so on. That is, after calling it you will have five new variables.

 Be careful while calling the `getDimensions` function, as they are assigned parameters following that predefined order, and not by name (you cannot call `getDimensions(channels,slices,height,width,frames)` and expect the result to be consistent with the variable names).

A note on slices, frames, and channels

As you may have noted, the coordinates for width and height of a given image start at 0. An image with a matrix size of 100 x 200 will have the x coordinate ranging from 0 to 99 and y coordinate from 0 to 199. However, the notation for slices, frames, and channels is different, as they always start at 1. Consider the following macro:

```
run("T1 Head (2.4M, 16-bits)");
for(i = 1; i<= nSlices; i++) {
  Stack.setSlice(i);
  value = getPixel(100, 100);
  print("Pixel (100, 100) in slice", i, "=", value);
  wait(200); // Wait 200 miliseconds
}
```

Let's stop for a moment on it, as it is using most of the concepts we have learned so far. First, it opens a sample image (`T1Head`) and then it uses a `for` loop to iterate through its slices using one of the `Stack` functions (take a look at the macro functions reference to see more stack operations). Note that the index variable used, `i`, starts at one and makes the loop run until (and including) its value is equal to `nSlices`. It then grabs the pixel value placed in the coordinates (`100, 100`) and prints it. When you run this macro, you will see how ImageJ goes through all the slices of the stack, and the pixel selected values printed in the log window. We have added a small waiting time (`200` milliseconds) as the parameter of the `wait` function, so that you can clearly see what is going on.

Try this: modify the preceding macro so that it only iterates through the even slices of the image. Also, try changing the starting loop value to 0. You would expect an error message, but it selects slice 1 instead. This may cause an incorrect measurement if you iterate a given image this way, as you will process the first slice twice!

Other useful `Stack` functions are `Stack.setFrame(frame)` and `Stack.setChannel(channel)`, which will allow you to select specific frames or channels, as we have just done with the slices.

There are two important aspects to be learned for running the preceding macro:

- The `getPixel(x,y)` function grabs the pixel value of the currently selected slice for the provided x and y coordinates. Note that the stack selection is done prior to getting the pixel value, and we are not providing any slice information to the `getPixel(x,y)` function.

- The macro system is deeply ingrained with the user interface. The results of the macro functions that affect an image in any given way (filtering, setting pixel values, changing the active slice / channel / frame, and so on) are shown on the screen immediately. Think of a macro as a very fast and efficient user performing the instructions you wrote down.

Selecting a specific image

Macro functions, unless specified, are applied to the image being displayed and selected, as we just saw. It may be the case that you have several images opened and want to apply different operations to each one of them or use information from one to modify another. There are several ways for selecting an opened image from the ImageJ macro language, which are as follows:

- Using the `selectImage(id)` function. This function is called with an argument that can mean two different things, depending on its value:
  - If it is a negative number, it is the image ID, an internal ImageJ number that is different for each image. This number is obtained by running `getImageID()`.
  - If it is a positive number, it is the order in which the images were opened. For instance, `selectImage(1)` will select the image that was opened before any other one, from the list of images currently opened (not really the first one in absolute terms, as the first image opened in that session could have been closed).

- Using the `selectWindow(name)` function, where `name` is a string that contains the window name you want to select.

The following macro opens two images and switches between them using all the approaches explained previously. We recommend running it line-by-line to understand how it works:

```
// Open two sample images.
run("Clown (14K)");
run("Leaf (36K)");
// How many images are there? You can also see this variable in the
debug window
print(nImages + " opened");
// Select the first opened image. This is the clown image, by opening
order.
selectImage(1);
// Is it really the clown image?
clownTitle = getTitle();
print("Image selected: " + clownTitle);
// Select an image by name
selectWindow(clownTitle);
// Get the image ID of the selected image. This is a negative number
that you normally do not
// know in advance (as opposed to the opening order number).
clownID = getImageID();
print("clown.jpg image ID: " + clownID);
// Select the leaf image (the second image opened).
selectImage(2);
// Go back to the clown image using the image ID, not the opening
order
selectImage(clownID);
```

Speeding up a macro

For complicated operations or processes that involve switching between several images, macros can be quite slow. The best way to speed up your macro is to use the `setBatchMode(arg)` function. This function stops ImageJ from displaying on the screen the operations being performed on the image, thus allowing the macro to run upto 20 times faster, according to the official documentation. This function receives an argument, which has to be `true` (for entering the batch mode) or `false` (for exiting it). When the macro finishes, the batch mode is set to `false` automatically.

You have to run `setBatchMode(true)` before opening the image or the images you wish to process to enjoy this speed bump. Setting it after the images are being processed and shown on the screen will have no impact on its execution.

You also have the option of programming a plugin or use some scripting language instead of a macro. Plugins are a more advanced topic that will be covered in the final two chapters of this book, and they generally require you to have some programming skills. Scripts are not covered in this book, but if you have knowledge in Python, for instance, you might want to take a look at them.

Adding a GUI to your macro

Sometimes you may want to try different values for some parameters without having to edit the macro code again and again in order to change the hardcoded variables. The `Dialog` functions allow you to build your own user interfaces to query the user for information before running the macro. A dialog is built by calling `Dialog.create(title)` and then adding the different elements that compose the user interface: textboxes for strings/numbers, sliders, selection menus, checkboxes, and radio buttons. Once all the elements are in place, we just need to get the user input and proceed with the processing of the macro.

The following code creates a simple dialog and will allow us to explore the possibilities of the dialog building functions with some additional nicety:

```
// We are using some relatively new functions, so we have to
// explicitly forbid this macro from running in old ImageJ versions
requires("1.47r");
// Create the main window with its title
Dialog.create("This is a test dialog");
// Grab two strings using a box 20 characters wide
Dialog.addString("String 1:", "First string", 20);
Dialog.addString("String 2:", "Second string", 20);
// And a number
Dialog.addNumber("Number:", 0);
// And a slider from 0 to 10, centered in 3
Dialog.addSlider("Slider:", 0, 10, 3);
// And a checkbox (checked)
Dialog.addCheckbox("Checkbox", true);
// And a radio button group with 3 rows and 2 columns,
// mark "2.0" as the default option
rboptions = newArray(1, 2, 3, 4, 5, 6);
Dialog.addRadioButtonGroup("Radio buttons", rboptions, 3, 2, "2.0");
// Finally, show the dialog on screen
Dialog.show();
// We are done building, now we need to get the values when the user
// clicks OK.
```

```
// We use the Dialog.get functions in the same order used
// to place the elements on the dialog.
s1 = Dialog.getString();
s2 = Dialog.getString();
n1 = Dialog.getNumber();
slider1 = Dialog.getNumber();
c1 = Dialog.getCheckbox();
b1 = Dialog.getRadioButton();
// Print all
print(s1, s2, n1, slider1, c1, b1);
```

When you run this macro, you will get a dialog similar to the following one, if everything went right:

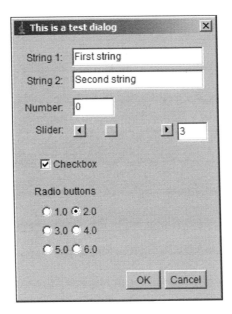

If the user clicks on **Cancel**, the window closes and the macro will not be executed. If the user clicks on **OK**, the variables are assigned and the macro continues its execution. In this case, it just prints the values on the screen one after the other.

Note the first line of the macro: the `requires(version)` function allows the macro to be run in versions newer than (and including) the one provided as an argument. It is a nice way of notifying the user, the need for updating the version before running a macro that may potentially not work in older versions.

If you only need to get one number or one string, you can skip most of these steps and simply call one of these special functions: `getNumber(message,defaultvalue)`, `getString(message,defaultvalue)`, where `message` is the text the user will see on the screen and `defaultvalue` is the initial value in the textbox. You do not need to call `Dialog.create(title)` before running any of these functions.

The batch mode

One common operation you will probably need to do at some point is to apply a macro to a large number of images. You have an option of using the `setBatchMode(arg)` function and code the logic for opening and closing each file. However, there is a simpler way of accomplishing this, which is just navigating to the **Process | Batch | Macro...** menu option. When you run it you will get a dialog similar to the following one:

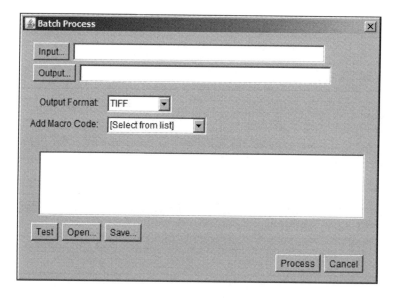

This dialog will allow you to apply a macro to all the images contained inside a given folder (**Input...**) and will store the result into another one (**Output...**) with the image format selected in the **Output Format** option. If you leave the output folder field empty, nothing will be saved (you may want to do this if your macro consists of a list of measurements and does not involve any image modification). You can write your macro code in the textbox or in an open (**Open...**) one that you have coded previously. The **Test** button runs the macro on the first image of the input directory and shows the result on the screen.

Imagine a possible application: we want to measure the number of tuberculosis bacilli in a folder containing 300 images. Now we have a very fast way of doing that precisely.

 You don't need to do any opening or closing of an image within your macro code while using this batch mode. Just consider that the image has been opened and selected for you when the macro starts. You only need to implement the necessary image processing tasks.

Installing macros for easy access

When you write a macro and save it to a file, you can run it easily by navigating to **Plugins** | **Macros** | **Run...**, and then select the file that contains it. However, if you are going to run a macro several times, this can get tiresome. Fortunately, you can install a set of macros for easy access by navigating to **Plugins** | **Macros** | **Install....** In order to use this command, we first have to give our macro a name. This is done in the following way:

```
macro "Test macro" {
// The macro code goes inside the curly braces. Nothing else changes.
}
```

You can have several macros in a file using this naming convention. Variables can be shared between different macros if they are defined outside the macro blocks and are preceded by the `var` keyword. Functions defined outside a particular macro block can be accessed by any macro in the file.

We will further explain these concepts with the following example:

```
var common = "I'm a common variable";
// This function can be called by either macro
functionmyprint(s) {
print(s);
}
macro "Macro 1" {
  macro1 = "I'm a variable that belongs to macro1";
  myprint(common); // Accesses a common variable using a common
function, that's OK
  myprint(macro1);
}
macro "Macro 2" {
    macro2 = macro1; // Will show an error message
}
```

Save this macro to a file by navigating to **Plugins | Macros | Install...**. Select the file you just saved and apparently nothing will happen, but the macros you have created are now accessible directly by navigating to the **Plugins | Macros** menu, below the divider bar. If you install another file containing macros, the previous ones will be replaced.

You can also assign key shortcuts to your macros. Simply add the key you want to use between the square brackets after the macro name, as follows:

```
macro "Macro 3 [m]" { ... }
```

If you install your macros and restart ImageJ, you will see that they are no longer there. You need to install them again to be able to access them quickly. If you want to have them accessible when you restart, you will need to add them to the ImageJ/macros/StartupMacros.txt file. This file is loaded every time ImageJ starts. You can browse for it or navigate to **Plugins | Macros | StartupMacros...**. This will open an editor window that will allow you to modify that file.

Shared macros – the ImageJ macro directory

Last but not the least: while learning a new programming technique, it is important to practise it by your own, but it is also very helpful to read code written by others so that you can see how most common operations are done and can understand new ways of doing things. There are dozens of macros contributed by the ImageJ users available at http://rsbweb.nih.gov/ij/macros/. We encourage you to take a look at the text files in that directory as it is an incredibly rich resource.

Summary

In this chapter, we have learned how to record a sequence of ImageJ operations into a macro that can be reused later on either for reproducing the same results or for processing a large number of images. We have also introduced macro programming, learning basic syntax and operators. These commands combined with the recorder output, will allow you to write a faster and more powerful code than what you would expect.

5
ImageJ Plugins for Users

The previous chapter explored the power of the ImageJ macro language and taught you how to create your own macros without much effort using the internal macro recorder, including some more in-depth programming operations. Now we will make a qualitative jump and will explain the ImageJ plugins, that are a versatile system for extending ImageJ, and will allow you to perform analytic tasks beyond the possibilities of the standard ImageJ distribution. This chapter includes:

- General concepts of ImageJ plugins
- How to install a plugin
- A brief selection of plugins you may find useful

ImageJ plugins

As we saw in the previous chapter, a macro is a series of ImageJ core functions that are executed sequentially in order to automate the analysis processes. While one of the main strengths of the macro system is that new macros can be produced without the need of prior programming experience, they are constrained within the ImageJ native capabilities and can also be quite slow.

However, ImageJ was built with extensibility in mind. It allows external Java classes to use its internal methods through a very well-documented public **Application Programming Interface (API)** available at `http://rsbweb.nih.gov/ij/developer/api/`. An Image plugin can, for instance, implement the necessary functions for reading and/or writing a type of file format that is initially not supported by ImageJ. It can carry on more sophisticated analysis, acquire images from external hardware or, in general, compute any mathematical operation involving images that you can think about. If you can code it in Java, ImageJ will handle the images for you, so now you only need to concentrate on solving the algorithmic part of your problem.

This is one of the reasons for ImageJ's success: it is easy to extend its capabilities and adapt it to your particular needs. As you will see in the next sections, there are quite a lot of plugins that have been contributed by developers to the ImageJ user community, so if you are looking for some extra functionality, no matter how specific, it is likely that all or part of your work is already been done.

Installing a plugin

Installing ImageJ plugins just requires you to download the plugin file (or files) and copy it into the `plugins/` directory that can be found inside the ImageJ's installation directory. After copying the file and restarting ImageJ, the plugin can be run from the corresponding **Plugins** menu option. The specific menu option depends on the plugin you have installed and sometimes on the path into which the file or files are being copied.

First of all, let's take a look at the **Plugins** menu structure. At the top of it, you will see some commands that you should already be familiar with (the ones related to macro development). Then there is a horizontal separation bar and several submenus (**3D**, **Analyze**, and so on). Now go to your ImageJ's installation directory and check the contents of the `plugins/` subdirectory. There is an almost perfect match between the directory listing of that folder and the options from the **Plugins** menu below the divider line:

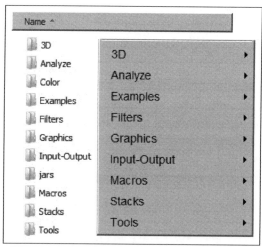

The contents of the `plugins/` folder along with the contents of the Plugins menu.

Please note that the `Color` folder is empty (or it was in our ImageJ installation at the time we took this screenshot), that is why it does not appear in the menu structure, and the `jars` folder is a container of external libraries and is not shown in the **Plugins** menu despite containing some files.

As you can see, the ImageJ **Plugins** menu replicates the structure of the `ImageJ/` `plugins` directory tree. That will help you to keep your plugins organized, as you can create your own folder structure. This will not work for all plugins, as some of them will internally define their position inside the menu structure, sometimes even outside the **Plugins** menu.

 As a matter of fact, many ImageJ menu commands are actually implemented as plugins.

Let's try installing a plugin on our own. One easy example is the `Text Demo` plugin. This is a very simple program that is used to show how text can be added to an image. It can be downloaded from `http://rsb.info.nih.gov/ij/plugins/` `text-demo.html`. In general, all plugins are installed in the same way, but you are encouraged to read the specific instructions written by the plugin developer, as some of them will require you to do something beyond just copying the file to the `plugins/` folder. In any case, this plugin is easy to install: just download the `Text_` `Demo.class` file (not the `.java` one) to the `plugins/` folder. When we restart ImageJ, we will find a new command when we navigate to **Plugins | Text Demo**. It is placed there, since we copied the file directly to the `plugins/` folder. We could also have copied it to some of the existing subfolders, or we could have created our own. If you run that command, you should see a window similar to the following one:

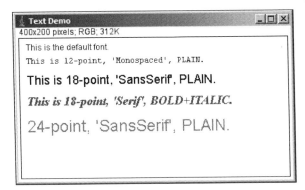

So that's it. You have just run your first ImageJ plugin downloaded from an external source. This is a simple example that shows how the different font styles can be used, but the ImageJ plugin system allows external developers (and you after reading the next chapter and some experience) to add almost any kind of functionality.

In the following section, we will cite some plugins which we have found especially useful, or are familiar with, or even those which have helped in developing. We hope you can find here some extension that suits your needs when you are facing some complex analysis.

Some useful plugins

Most of the plugins listed in this section have been obtained from
`http://rsb.info.nih.gov/ij/plugins/index.html`, which at the time
of writing hosted about 500 of them. This is consequently only a small subset
of those, but we hope our selection allows you to understand how versatile
ImageJ can be. Please note that the following sections are not a brief user manual,
as even a small set of instructions for each plugin would take a lot of space.
Consider them just as a personal compilation to have a taste of what can be
accomplished by using different plugins.

LOCI Bio-Formats

As we commented in the second chapter, there are a number of image formats that
ImageJ can read natively. There are plugins that allow it to read other formats, and
indeed the original installation package includes several of them by default under
the `plugins/Input-Output` folder.

One particular powerful plugin for file input and output operations is the **Laboratory
for Optical and Computational Instrumentation (LOCI)**, a biophotonics research
laboratory at the University of Wisconsin-Madison. The Bio-Formats library allows
us to read and write several dozens of different imaging formats with different levels
of support, depending on the specific format. The entire list of supported formats can
be accessed from `http://loci.wisc.edu/software/bio-formats`. The good thing
about this library for us, ImageJ users, is that it is also offered as an ImageJ plugin
(`http://loci.wisc.edu/bio-formats/imagej`). When this plugin is installed, a
LOCI menu will appear. We can then use this plugin's capabilities to open a greater
number of different formats.

Another great thing about this plugin is that we can use it in our own macros or
plugins, so if we are working with formats unsupported in the raw version of
ImageJ, we can still automate our analysis procedures.

Image segmentation

The term image segmentation refers to the general concept of dividing the image
into regions of interest and background elements we do not want to measure. There
exist many different methods for doing this, and in fact the simple act of drawing a
rectangular selection over the image is itself a form of segmentation. Some ImageJ
plugins allow us to perform more fine-grained selections or run semi-automatic
processes based on prior learning.

Auto Threshold and Auto Local Threshold

In the previous chapters, we learned that objects in the image can be segmented by classifying background or object pixels depending on their level of intensity (thresholding). There are several methods for calculating this threshold automatically. If you want to display in a single step, the result of applying every method on your image, use the plugin called Auto Threshold (`http://fiji.sc/wiki/index.php/Auto_Threshold`), which will create a montage with the result of automatic thresholding with every available method applied to your image. One limitation of these methods is that they calculate a global threshold that is the same for all pixels in the image. Other methods apply a different threshold for every pixel, based on the surrounding values (this is called local thresholding). You can also test all the available local thresholding methods on your image in a single step with the Auto Local Threshold plugin (`http://fiji.sc/Auto_Local_Threshold`).

The trainable Weka segmentation

This plugin uses the Weka machine learning library (`http://www.cs.waikato.ac.nz/ml/weka/`) and allows ImageJ to perform segmentation operations through machine learning techniques. It can be downloaded from `http://fiji.sc/Trainable_Weka_Segmentation`. In that same page there are instructions for working with it, but if we summarize them, it is a two-step process:

1. Train the classifier. You will have to manually segment your image and assign the different regions to different classes (two are created by default, but you can add more) and then click on the **Train classifier** button. So then it learns the features of the different classes. By default, it uses a random forest method, but several more are available.

2. Once the classifier has been trained, you can apply it to other similar images to obtain the proposed segmentation.

SIOX (Simple Interactive Object Extraction)

SIOX (`http://www.siox.org/`) is an advanced algorithm used to extract the foreground objects in an image from the background elements that are of no interest. It works in a similar way to the previous plugin: the user needs to train the method using the native ImageJ ROI tools, so that it can learn which elements should be considered foreground and which ones background. The plugin then proceeds to isolate the objects that we consider relevant and creates a mask that can be applied to the original image to remove the background. The trained classifier can be saved, as in the case of the Weka tool, in order to apply it to several similar images.

Clustering

There are also a number of plugins that help to segment an image using unsupervised machine learning techniques. These methods try to separate automatically the different image regions based on the pixel values without the need for user intervention. Two of these plugins are k-means clustering (`http://ij-plugins.sourceforge.net/plugins/segmentation/k-means.html`), which can be used for static images, or jClustering (`https://github.com/HGGM-LIM/jclustering`), which is intended as a framework for the implementation of unsupervised clustering algorithms for dynamic images (2D + time or 3D + time) and groups image regions according to their time activities.

Image registration

This is the process of aligning two or more images so that the corresponding features can easily be related. If you have two images that represent the same object in the real world but seem to appear with different parameters (acquisition technique differs or sample has been imaged at two time points), you can try synchronizing both windows by navigating to **Analyze | Tools | Synchronize Windows**, but the coordinates will not match if they are not properly aligned. This alignment process is called image registration, and it consists of calculating the geometrical transformation that has to be applied to one of the images to be aligned to the other.

Geometrical transformations are divided in two main groups: linear and non-linear. A geometrical transformation modifies the coordinates of the pixels in your image, so it changes pixel positions in space. If the transformation applied to an image is linear, that means that the straight lines in the image will still be straight after the transformation. Non-linear ones, on the other hand, have no restrictions on how pixel coordinates are modified, so straight lines could be transformed into curves. You may be thinking why do you need to know all this. The answer is that depending on your registration problem, a different transformation maybe the right solution. The following diagram shows different types of linear transformations:

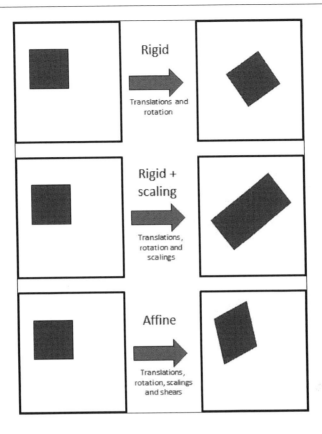

The linear transformations in the diagram are sorted from less to more parameters involved. A rigid transformation only allows translating and rotating the image, we can then add scaling (that can be different in every direction) and also shears (also one in every direction). If you try to align two images of the same object in which the acquisition device is just displaced, a rigid transformation may be enough. If the distance from the sample to the camera has changed between acquisitions, you may need to apply some scaling, and if the sample has been deformed in one of the images, a linear transformation won't be enough, and you will have to look for a non-linear one.

If image registration is the process of finding the geometrical transformation necessary to align the images, registration plugins will try to help you in this searching process. They can do this automatically or manually. Automatic image registration will measure if images are correctly aligned (with a function called similarity measure) and will modify the geometric transformation in an iterative process until the value for the similarity measure is the maximum. All this process is transparent to the user. Manual registration plugins will ask the user for some features in both the images and calculate the transformation that aligns those points. Let's take a look at one example of the first type.

Stackreg

This plugin (available from `http://bigwww.epfl.ch/thevenaz/stackreg/`) aligns a stack of images, using every image in the stack as a template to align the next one. You also need to install a second plugin called Turboreg (`http://bigwww.epfl.ch/thevenaz/turboreg/`), since it provides functions used by Stackreg.

From the previous chapters you know that an image stack can represent a 3D object, so every 2D image represents a slice of that object. Imagine you acquire every slice as an independent picture, and consequently you were not able to place every 2D slice of your sample exactly in the same position as in the previous one. The resulting stack will have the images misaligned when the Z coordinate changes. This plugin is the right one to solve this problem.

If you want to test how Stackreg works, load the test image called `tuberculosis_stack_unreg.tif`. You will probably notice that there is something wrong with this image: the three color channels are not correctly aligned (open `tuberculosis.tif` to compare with the original image if you don't believe this). Stackreg can solve this problem, but it accepts a stack as input and not a multichannel image. You can convert this example image into a stack by navigating to **Image | Color | Split Channels** (three images are created) and then by navigating to **Image | Stacks | Images to Stack**. Now select this new stack and run Stackreg. You only need to select the type of transformation that the registration algorithm will look for. In this example, the images are only translated. So translation would be enough. If you select a transformation with more parameters than needed, the worst that could happen is that the solution is incorrect, so better select the simplest transformation that matches your problem. After you click on **OK**, the plugin will run and when finished (less than one minute) the misaligned stack will be substituted by an aligned one. You can check whether the result is correct by creating again a composite image by navigating to **Image | Colors | Make Composite**.

3D volume rendering

Displaying stack data with the **Orthogonal Views** tool (accessible by navigating to the **Image | Stacks** menu) is helpful when trying to explore your 3D data data. But if you want a 3D representation of your data that you can interact with, Volume Viewer is your plugin.

Volume Viewer

Although this plugin is already installed in ImageJ distribution, we recommend you download the latest version (`http://rsbweb.nih.gov/ij/plugins/volume-viewer.html`), as the improvements are worth it. You need to delete the old version from your `plugins` folder before copying the new one, or ImageJ will complain about duplicities. Load the sample image **T1 head** and navigate to **Plugins | 3D | Volume Viewer** in order to test the plugin. Any volume rendering technique creates a two dimensional image from your 3D data by passing rays through your image, and applying some function to the pixel values that the ray encounters in its trip. Depending on your data, the proper values for that function may be difficult to set.

Volume Viewer has several modes for creating the render. **Slice** and **Slice & Borders** do not pass any rays through your 3D data, they just create a slice with unrestricted orientation, and you can modify this orientation by clicking and moving the mouse on the 3D display. **Max projection** and **Projection** are real rendering modes, since the value of the final image will be the maximum or the sum of all the pixels encountered by every ray. These modes are not especially interesting for our sample image (that is a magnetic resonance study), but are very useful if we are interested in very bright pixels in our data or if the sum of all the pixel values is meaningful, as for instance in computed tomography. Finally, the **Volume** mode is the one that offers more possibilities. There are many options that you can play with. We will give you some initial help on the basics:

- **Distance** is used to select part of your original volume to be used in the rendering process. If you set it to the minimum value, the whole stack will be used.

- The **Scale** parameter zooms in or out your 3D view.

- The main parameter in order to change the way your volume render is created is the alpha value in **Transfer Function** (the orange line in the plot on the right). It indicates the transparency of every pixel depending on its intensity. Pixels with low intensity values are usually more transparent (low alpha), while those pixels with high intensity values are more opaque (high alpha). You can modify this behavior with the mouse.

- You can also add some **Light** to your 3D view, with several parameters that will affect the result.

The following screenshot shows the **T1 head** image loaded and rendered in the **Volume** mode. Some parameters have been modified from the default values: scale has been increased, alpha values have been modified (low intensity values are completely transparent), and light has been turned on:

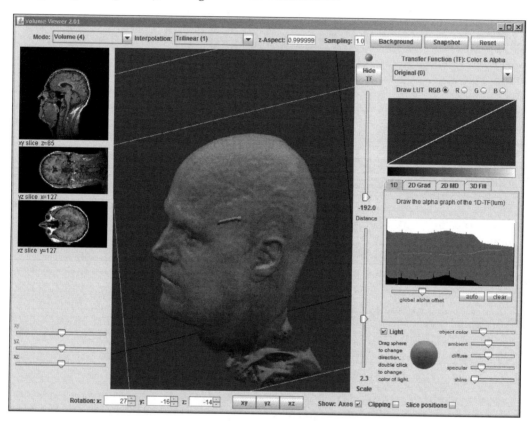

Other utilities

There are ImageJ plugins available for almost every operation you can perform on an image. Some of them do not fit in the preceding categories, so in this section we present a brief list of other plugins that we have found to be useful or are excellent examples of the adaptability of ImageJ.

MosaicJ

MosaicJ (`http://bigwww.epfl.ch/thevenaz/mosaicj/`) implements the necessary algorithms to perform image stitching, that is, the composition of a mosaic from individual images.

FigureJ

ImageJ is so versatile that some of the plugins serve for purposes you would not have imagined. FigureJ (`http://imagejdocu.tudor.lu/doku.php?id=plugin:utilities:figurej:start`) is an ImageJ plugin designed to ease the sometimes tedious job of preparing figures for scientific publications.

Study anonymization

For those of us working with medical images, the removal of a patient's data is a very important step prior to sharing or processing images. There are several ImageJ plugins that remove sensitive information from the DICOM headers. Two of them are DICOM Rewriters (`http://rsb.info.nih.gov/ij/plugins/dicom-rewriter.html`) and others are Anonymize IJ DICOM (`http://rsbweb.nih.gov/ij/plugins/anonymize-ij-dicom/index.html`).

 We are only listing these plugins here as an example to prove what ImageJ can do. We are not encouraging their use in any way, so if you are going to use them to anonymize your studies, please first check that the resulting files do not contain any sensitive information.

FIJI (Fiji Is Not ImageJ)

This last item deserves a section on its own. You might have found interesting some of the plugins that we showed you previously, and might be willing to try them on your sample images. If that is the case, you would have to download and install every one of them individually in your system. If you want to try many different plugins, this can take some time.

Fortunately for us, there is a solution, **Fiji (Fiji Is Just ImageJ)** is an ImageJ distribution, much alike Linux distributions, which includes the core ImageJ functionalities, in addition to many extra plugins, an auto-updating system and some extra niceties. You can access the entire list of included plugins at `http://fiji.sc/Category:Plugins`.

You can download and install Fiji from `http://fiji.sc/Downloads`. Choose the right version for your operating system and unpack the compressed file to the folder of your choice. Inside, you will see the Fiji's executable file. Below you can see the main ImageJ and Fiji windows one on top of another. They are virtually the same, but notice the number of Fiji commands printed on its status bar:

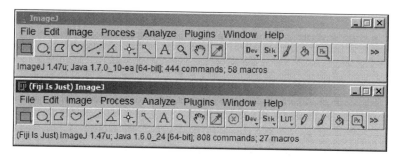

If you install it, try the different menu options. You will see that there are many more than in ImageJ, as the plugins it includes are distributed among the different menus, not only in the **Plugins** one. Also, try creating a new macro (by navigating to **Plugins | New | Macro...**). The Fiji editor is much more flexible than the basic ImageJ editor, as it has syntax coloring and many other features that make macro editing, a much pleasant experience. Everything we have explained about ImageJ so far can be done with Fiji in exactly the same way.

Summary

In this chapter, you have learned what an ImageJ plugin is and how to download and install whatever tool you need. In the next chapter, we will see how to code your own plugins, which are much more powerful than macros, but require more programming knowledge.

6
ImageJ Plugins for Developers

In the previous chapter you saw how to install a plugin that is available for download from the developer website. We also introduced some of them that are potentially useful in a wide range of applications. This chapter includes the following:

- A brief description of ImageJ plugin architecture with examples
- A walk through some common operations
- A guide for developing ImageJ plugins using the Eclipse IDE

This chapter will require prior programming experience, ideally with Java, but there is nothing here outside the concepts handled by other object oriented programming languages.

A sample plugin

We will start digging into this topic by analyzing the following plugin code. That will give us a nice starting point to introduce the different aspects for developing ImageJ plugins:

```
import ij.*;
import ij.process.*;
import ij.gui.*;
import java.awt.*;
import ij.plugin.*;
import ij.plugin.frame.*;

public class Test_Plugin implements PlugIn {
```

```
    public void run(String arg) {
        int width = 300;
        int height = 300;
    ImageProcessor ip = new ByteProcessor(width, height);
    ip.setColor(Color.black);
        ip.fill();
        for(int x = 0; x < width; x++) {
        for(int y = 0; y < height; y++) {
          if (x == y || (width - x) == y)
             ip.putPixel(x, y, 255);
        }
      }
      ImagePlus imp = new ImagePlus("Result image", ip);
      imp.show();
    }
  }
```

First things first: this is a plugin, and not a macro. To edit it, navigate to **Plugins | New | Plugin**. A sample skeleton will be opened and you just need to fill in the run(arg) method (previously, delete the example code that is inside it). When you are done, save the plugin in the ImageJ plugins folder of your working ImageJ installation. The editor is smart enough to change the name of your class to match the name of the file, as Java requires. Also, your class name must contain at least one underscore (_), or ImageJ will not find it. Remember to use the .java extension for the file.

> For advanced users: if you build a JAR file and place inside it plugins. config file that defines which classes are plugins, then there is no need of underscore in the name. In any case, this option is outside the scope of this book, but we wanted to place this warning here, so that you do not think that the underscore is always mandatory.

After completing these steps, you will have a .java file in your plugins folder. Now you need to compile it so that ImageJ can run it. This is done from the editing window, by navigating to **File | Compile** and then **Run** (*Ctrl* + *R*). If you do not have a Java Development Kit installed in your computer, then ImageJ will offer to download the Compiler.jar plugin, which will allow you to compile new plugins without the need to modify your Java installation. Click on **OK** on the dialog that shows up if that happens, as you will need it.

If everything has gone according to the plan, now you will also have a
Test_Plugin.class file in your plugins folder, and the following
screenshot will be displayed:

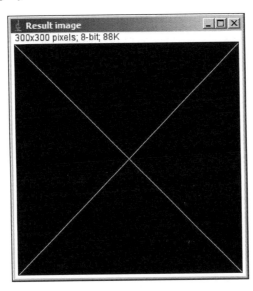

We have just run our first ImageJ plugin developed by ourselves. This time, we
had to do it from the **Compile** and **Run** menu options in the editor window. As the
.class file is now in your plugins folder, the next time you restart ImageJ you will
see a **Test Plugin** option in the **Plugin** menu in the main ImageJ window. Let's go
through the code in small chunks, so that you understand what we are doing.

You can also find your plugin in the ImageJ menus without the need of
a restart if you navigate to **Help | Refresh Menus**. Throughout this text,
we will always speak of restarting ImageJ, but bear in mind that you can
always use this option.

The first lines include all the necessary library imports and are added automatically
by the ImageJ proposed skeleton. If you need to use some other library, put your
import here. Then we declare our Test_Plugin class, which implements an interface
called PlugIn. There are several ways to code ImageJ plugins, depending on which
interface we are implementing, but in this book we are going to focus on two of
them: PlugIn and PlugInFilter. Depending on the purpose of our plugin,
we will be using one or the other.

The `PlugIn` interface needs us to implement just one method, `run(String arg)`, that is immediately executed when the plugin is run. The `PlugInFilter` needs two methods, `setup(String arg, ImagePlus imp)` and `run(ImageProcessor ip)`. The `setup` method is the first one that is being run and checks whether the image to which the plugin is being applied (the `ImagePlus` object passed as reference) has certain properties. Note that we are ignoring the `String arg` parameter, as it is outside the scope of this book and is not really needed to build powerful plugins. We can make the following distinction: a `PlugIn` interface implementation can be run in a standalone fashion and the `PlugInFilter` is applied to an already opened image, just similar to what a macro does. This is a very rough division but it is the one we will use in this book. We will work a bit with the `PlugInFilter` interface next in this section. For now, let's keep going through our code.

In the `run` method of our example we create a new square (300 x 300) `ImageProcessor` object. This is an abstract class that needs to be instantiated depending on the type of image we want to use. In this case, as we are working with a simple 8-bit image, we create a `ByteProcessor` object with `width` and `height` as parameters. We can also use a `ShortProcessor` object (16-bit unsigned data), `BinaryProcessor` (similar to `ByteProcessor`, but its pixel values can only take two values: 0 or 255), `FloatProcessor` (32-bit floating point values), or `ColorProcessor` (32-bit RGB image). Once the `ImageProcessor` object has been created, we can start using its methods to modify its pixel values.

The next thing we do is to set the color chooser to black (`ip.setColor(Color.black)`) and fill the current ROI with it (`ip.fill()`). As we have not defined any ROI, this method fills the whole image with the black color.

Next we create two nested `for` loops (one for the x axis, another for the y axis) and iterate through all the image pixels, by setting those belonging to either diagonal with the `ip.putPixel(x, y, value)` method to 255.

If you work with a `FloatProcessor` object, use the `putPixelValue` method that accepts a `double` value as the `value` parameter type.

After this step, the actual processing is finished. All that is left is to create an `ImagePlus` object with a title and the pixel contents of the `ImageProcessor` object and show it on the screen. An `ImagePlus` object also contains the image's metadata, such as the spatial scale or the calibration. Note that the `run` method for this interface does not return anything. You must compute all the resulting images and show them on the screen.

In summary, the philosophy of ImageJ plugin development is to treat ImageJ as an imaging processing library (ij.jar and all its contents), and as a platform that takes care of all the common nuisances (image reading, displaying, saving, and so on) associated with image processing.

The PlugInFilter interface

As we said before, the PlugInFilter interface is the one you need to implement if you want to code a plugin that performs operations on an image that is already open (similar to what macros do). This interface provides an extra method (setup) for you to implement that checks whether the image to be acted upon is of the type expected by the plugin and then proceeds to execute the run method. The following plugin offers an example and will also serve to explain additional functions:

```java
import ij.*;
import ij.process.*;
import ij.gui.*;
import java.awt.*;
import ij.plugin.filter.*;

public class Example_Filter_Plugin implements PlugInFilter {

    ImagePlus imp;

    public int setup(String arg, ImagePlus imp) {
      boolean wrong_version = IJ.versionLessThan("1.46r");
      if (wrong_version)
        return DONE;

      this.imp = imp;
      return DOES_8G;
    }

    public void run(ImageProcessor ip) {
      IJ.showStatus("Start processing...");
      IJ.wait(2000);
      int height = ip.getHeight();
      int width = ip.getWidth();
      for (int x = 0; x < width; x++) {
        for(int y = 0; y < height; y++) {
          int val = ip.getPixel(x, y);
          if (val > 100)
            ip.putPixel(x, y, val/10);
```

```
          }
        }
      }
    }
```

As we did in the previous example, let's go through this piece of code carefully to understand what it does, skipping the imports section, class name, and the interface implementation.

The first thing to notice is that there is a reference to an `ImagePlus` object within this class. This reference is assigned within the `setup` method, which serves in part as a constructor. We may need this reference during the call to the `run` method.

In the `setup` method, we have added a call to `IJ.versionLessThan(version)`. The `IJ` class offers static utility methods. If the ImageJ's version running the plugin is lower than the one specified, an error message pops up and the function returns `true`. If that is the case, we return the `DONE` static constant. Else, we assign the reference to our `ImagePlus` object and return `DOES_8G`.

These static constants are defined inside the `PlugInFilter` class and are used to define the behavior the plugin will have and the type of images it will handle. The following table summarizes some of them:

Constant	Meaning
DOES_16, DOES_32, DOES_8C, DOES_8G, DOES_RGB, DOES_ALL	The plugin analyzes images with 16-bit, 32-bit, 8-bit color (LUT), 8-bit grayscale, RGB data or everything
DONE	The plugin returns and skips the run method
DOES_STACKS	The run method is automatically repeated for each slice of the stack
STACK_REQUIRED	The plugin requires a stack
NO_UNDO	The final result cannot be undone (*Ctrl* + *Z*)
ROI_REQUIRED	The plugin needs an ROI drawn over the image to work

These constants can be combined (for instance, DOES_16 + DOES_STACKS + STACK_REQUIRED causes the plugin to analyze 16-bit stacks and check whether the image is indeed a stack.) In the preceding example, the returned constant is DOES_8G, which means that the plugin will work only on 8-bit grayscale images. If you try to run it on an image of a different type, will get an error message informing about the type of image this plugin can handle.

The `run` method is similar to the one you saw previously. In this case, it finds the pixels with a value greater than 100 and divides them by 10 (using the `getPixel(x, y)` and `setPixel(x, y, value)` methods). Note that we did not need to create an `ImageProcessor` object, as it was taken from the current image and passed to our method as an argument. In case the original image is a stack and the `DOES_STACKS` constant has been returned during the setup stage, the `run` method is executed once for each slice, and the `ImageProcessor` object corresponds to a different slice each time.

When you save, compile, and run your plugin as we did previously with the `tuberculosis_sample.tif` image opened, you will get the following result:

Oooops! As we said before, this is what will happen when you try to use a `PlugInFilter` interface with an unsupported image type. You will get this error message and the plugin will not run. Happily, we can transform image types easily by navigating to **Image | Type | 8-bit**. We can also modify the code so that the `setup` method returns `DOES_8G + DOES_16`. In any case, after running the image type conversion command, we can run our plugin again. The following is the result:

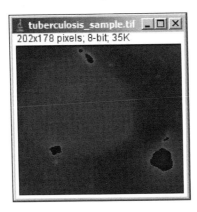

Note that we did not need to create and show a new image after the processing was finished, as the `PlugInFilter` interface modifies the currently selected image via the appropriate `ImageProcessor` methods.

Adding a GUI to your plugin

Just as we did while developing macros, there is a way to add a user interface to your plugin. This will allow us to ask the user for input regarding specific parameters that your code will use before running. This is done through methods of the `GenericDialog` class. Consider the following example, which will also introduce other concepts:

```
import ij.*;
import ij.process.*;
import ij.gui.*;
import java.awt.*;
import ij.plugin.filter.*;

public class Dialog_Example implements PlugInFilter {

    ImagePlus imp;
    boolean dialogCanceled = false;
    int radius = 3;
    int filterType;

    public int setup(String arg, ImagePlus imp) {
      this.imp = imp;
      return DOES_ALL;
    }

    public void run(ImageProcessor ip) {
      doDialog();
      if (dialogCanceled) return;
      RankFilters rf = new RankFilters();
      rf.rank(ip, radius, filterType);
    }

    private void doDialog() {
      GenericDialog gd = new GenericDialog("Dialog example");
      gd.addMessage("This is a sample generic dialog");
      gd.addChoice("Filter type: ", new String[]{"Mean", "Median"},
"Mean");
      gd.addNumericField("Input your filter width:", radius, 0);
      gd.showDialog();
      if (gd.wasCanceled()) {
        dialogCanceled = true;
      } else {
        String ch1 = gd.getNextChoice();
        if (ch1.equals("Mean"))
```

```
        filterType = RankFilters.MEAN;
      else if (ch1.equals("Median"))
      filterType = RankFilters.MEDIAN;
      radius = (int) gd.getNextNumber();
    }
  }
}
```

The preceding code opens a dialog and allows the user to select between two types of filtering (**Mean** or **Median**) and a filter radius. The selection is then applied to the current image. This is the dialog that we have created:

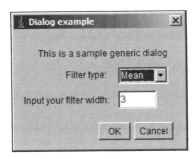

In the preceding code, the setup method is very simple. It simply assigns the ImagePlus reference and returns the DOES_ALL constant, which will allow us to use this plugin in every type of image. There are other variables declared in the class body and we will go through them in a second.

Before getting into the run() method, let's consider a new method added for this example, doDialog(). This method does not require any arguments and returns nothing. It is simply a helper method used to build the user interface. As said before, this is done by creating an instance of the GenericDialog class and then adding new components in a way very similar to what we did while building GUIs in a macro. In this case, we have added a message, a drop-down list, and a numeric field. After all the components have been added, we need to call the showDialog() method and then check whether the user clicked on the **Cancel** button. If that is the case, we set the dialogCanceled variable to true. As you can see, this variable is then checked in the run method and, if true, the plugin does nothing.

If the user doesn't cancel the dialog, then the variables will be recovered. As you can see, the choice in the drop-down menu is used to set the right value to the filterType variable according to the static constants defined in the RankFilters class. This class implements some of the ImageJ filters and is the one we will use for the actual filtering. The value of the radius variable is cast to the int data type, as the getNextNumber() method returns a double value.

After all the user input has been retrieved, all that is left to do is call the actual filtering on the `ImageProcessor` object, which the `run` method receives as an argument. This is done with the `rank` method of the `RankFilters` class with appropriate parameters.

Can we build the GUI in the `setup` method? There is nothing that prevents us from doing that, but consider this: This method is used to check whether the plugin can work with an active image. This check is done after the appropriate constants are returned. If we build the dialog here, the dialog will pop up even if there are no images open or if they are of the wrong type, which is a waste of time for the user if the plugin cannot be finally applied.

You can also create your GUI using AWT or swing components, but consider an advantage of using the `GenericDialog` class: It also makes your plugin macro-compatible. That is, when you use it and give it certain parameters, it will emit a line in the recorder that you can then use to automatize your process.

 Your plugin may have more than one class. Remember that ImageJ will only show those containing an underscore in their names under the **Plugins** menu. If you need helper classes, just do not use that symbol to avoid confusion with the actual plugin.

The ImageJ plugin API

As you have just seen in the previous example, there is a class that implements several filters, but the exact operation you want to implement will surely have to rely on many other classes. The best resource you can have at hand when coding a new ImageJ plugin is the ImageJ Java API, accessible at `http://rsbweb.nih.gov/ij/developer/api/`. This includes a list of all the classes and methods that can be used to develop your plugin.

We understand that this resource can be very arid at the beginning of your coding practices. Remember that reading code written by others is an excellent way of learning once you have a grip on the basics. A large number of plugins offered at `http://rsbweb.nih.gov/ij/plugins/index.html` also have their source code available. So, this is a great starting point to extend what you already know about plugin development.

Even though it is not the purpose of this book to offer an exhaustive list of all the classes and the operations they provide, in the following table we have listed some of them which are mostly used:

Operation	Relevant classes or methods
Filter	`RankFilters, Filters3D`
Open / Save image	`Opener, FileSaver, IJ.open(), IJ.save()`
Plot	`Plot`
Run macro	`IJ.runMacro(), IJ.runMacroFile()`
Histogram	`ImageProcessor.getHistogram()`
ROI handling	`ROI` (and its subclasses)
Measurements	`Measurements` interface and all the implementing classes and interfaces, especially `ImageStatistics`
Analyze Particles	`ParticleAnalyzer`
Get active image	`IJ.getImage()`
Get image IDs, get image by ID or name	`WindowManager.getIDList(), WindowManager.getImage()`
Capture mouse movements or clicks on the image	Add the appropriate AWT `Listeners` to the `ImageCanvas` object

Setting up ImageJ under the Eclipse IDE

Developing simple plugins for ImageJ can be accomplished with the default editor and a little effort. For more complex programs, the Fiji editor provides extra niceties (such as syntax coloring and more informative error messages). But the real breakthrough comes when combining the ImageJ plugin system and an advanced Java IDE. In this section, we will set up Eclipse (`http://www.eclipse.org/`) to work with ImageJ. This will allow us to write, debug, and run our plugins in a better way.

 Though we have chosen Eclipse for this section, the basics should be easily translated to other popular development environments, for example, NetBeans.

This section assumes that you already have a working Eclipse installation. If you do not have one, please go to `http://www.eclipse.org/ downloads/packages/eclipse-classic-422/junosr2` (the latest Eclipse version at the time of the writing) and follow the installation instructions for your platform.

Let's set up our system, by performing the following steps:

1. Open Eclipse and create a new project (navigating to **File | New | Java Project**).

2. Give it a name you want and store it in the folder of your choice; for this example we will call our project as `imagejexample`.

3. Have separate folders for its source and binary output, as it will be necessary later on (see in the following screenshot):

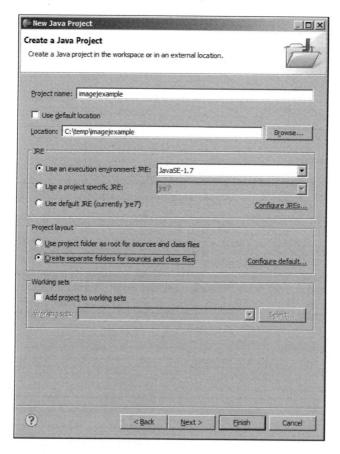

4. Click on **Next**.

While choosing the Java version you want to use to compile your project, remember that the bundled version of ImageJ comes with Java JRE 6.

In the next window, in the **Source** tab, choose `imagejexample/plugins` (instead of `imagejexamples/bin`) as the output folder. In the **Libraries** tab, you will have the common libraries for the JRE system library that you chose in the first step:

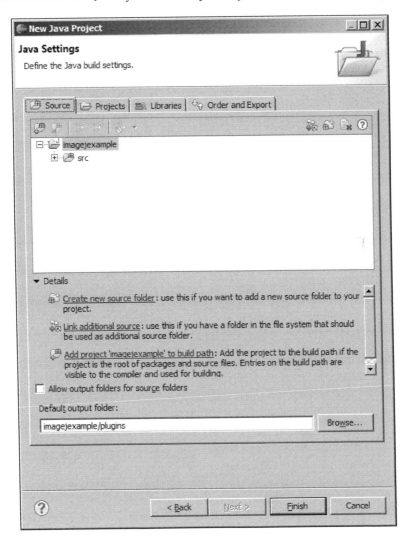

Now click on the **Add External JARs...** button and select the ij.jar file of your ImageJ installation. The following screenshot shows these tabs with their appropriate values. Click on **Finish** to and create your project:

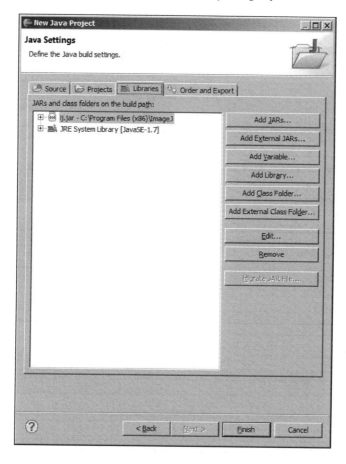

We are almost finished. Now you need to check whether your project is using the ImageJ's main class from the ij.jar file when it is run. You can do so by right-clicking on your project in the **Package Explorer** tab and then on **Properties...**. From there, select the **Run/Debug Settings** menu. You will see a configuration called **New_configuration** (if not, create a new one clicking on **New...** and the selecting **Java Application**), click on it and then on the **Edit...** button. In the window that shows up, in the **Main** tab, check whether ij.ImageJ has been entered in the **Main class** text field, as shown in the following screenshot:

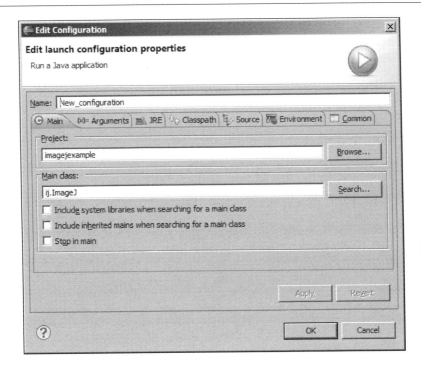

Eclipse may have done this for you, but it does not hurt to check. Click on **OK** and close all setup windows. We are done!

You can test if your setup is correct by clicking on your project name and then navigating to the **Run | Run** (*Ctrl + F11*) menu option. A new ImageJ window should pop up, and the **Plugins** menu should be empty below the divider bar. It is empty because this ImageJ version now expects to find the plugins within the specified output folder (where the .class files will be created). As it is currently empty (we have not started to code our own plugins under this system), there are no plugins to be shown.

Our first Eclipse ImageJ plugin

Now it is time to start coding our first plugin with the Eclipse configuration. Right-click on your project name and create a new class by navigating to the **New | Class** option. Implement the `PlugInFilter` interface in the class (clicking on the **Browse...** button and searching all the classes inside the `ij` package) and give it any name you want. Using the default package is fine, even though Eclipse displays a warning.

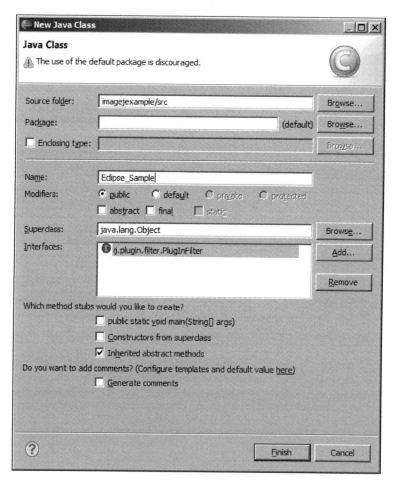

When you do this, you will have a new editor window with the following contents:

```
import ij.ImagePlus;
import ij.plugin.filter.PlugInFilter;
import ij.process.ImageProcessor;
```

```
public class Eclipse_Sample implements PlugInFilter {

    @Override
    public void run(ImageProcessor arg0) {
        // TODO Auto-generated method stub

    }

    @Override
    public int setup(String arg0, ImagePlus arg1) {
        // TODO Auto-generated method stub
        return 0;
    }

}
```

As you can see, Eclipse automatically creates the skeleton of your class for you and overrides the methods you need to implement. This skeleton is not as complete as the one that ImageJ provides when we create plugins from its menus, but it is fine. What is great about developing plugins in Eclipse is that now, for instance, we can autocomplete the code, as this environment has internal knowledge of the classes contained within the `ij.jar` file. As an example, when we are filling in the `setup` method we can ask it to complete the name of the constants which are to be returned (Eclipse will do it automatically for us as we type, or we can press *Ctrl* + Space bar), as shown in the following screenshot:

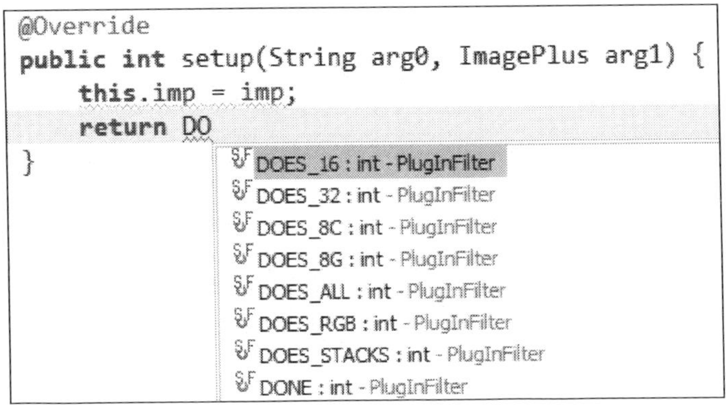

```
@Override
public int setup(String arg0, ImagePlus arg1) {
    this.imp = imp;
    return DO
}
           DOES_16 : int - PlugInFilter
           DOES_32 : int - PlugInFilter
           DOES_8C : int - PlugInFilter
           DOES_8G : int - PlugInFilter
           DOES_ALL : int - PlugInFilter
           DOES_RGB : int - PlugInFilter
           DOES_STACKS : int - PlugInFilter
           DONE : int - PlugInFilter
```

This also works for every method of every class inside the ImageJ package.

There is one more thing you can do to ease the development process: associate the ImageJ Javadoc (the API documentation) with the `ij.jar` file that is located in the `Referenced Libraries` folder in your project. Right-click on the filename and select **Properties**. In the window that appears, select **Javadoc Location** and add the API URL. You can check if the URL is the right one, by clicking on the **Validate...** button. If everything is correct, you should see the following screenshot:

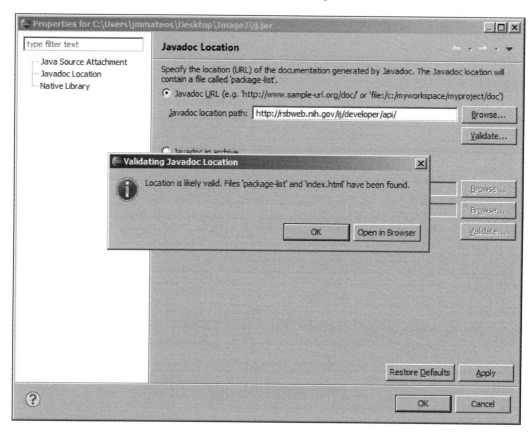

The autocomplete function is now more informative, as it is accompanied by the exact description of the code published in the API in a yellow box next to the selected method or constant:

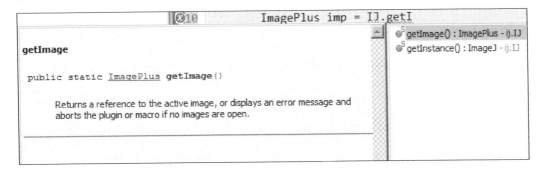

Sharing your plugin

So let's say you have coded your plugin and you want to give it to a colleague to use. You can give your .java files for all your classes, if you have more than one, but the final user will have to compile them. You can also send the .class files that will be placed in your plugins directory. One of the great things of Java is that a program compiled on a computer works on other systems as well. Just tell your colleague to copy the .class files to the plugins folder of his or her ImageJ installation.

Better yet: offer your plugin code through a popular code-sharing site, for example, https://github.com/. You will be helping the community and doing yourself a favor: someone might spot a bug in your code and report it, and in that case you can submit a corrected version.

Using external libraries

It may happen that using only the ImageJ and the Java native classes is not enough to accomplish what you want to do. Perhaps you need advanced mathematical functions, similar to the ones that can be found on the excellent Apache Commons Math library (http://commons.apache.org/proper/commons-math/). While you may think that you should implement every single mathematical algorithm that your plugin is going to use, code reutilization is encouraged here, as it is a good principle not to reinvent the wheel and use well-tested libraries that already provide some of the functions that you need. As you saw during the Eclipse setup phase, it is very easy to add an external library and start using the classes provided by it. But, if you do that, how can you distribute your plugin once it is done?

You might have noticed a `jars` folder inside the `plugins` folder. That folder contains the `.jar` (or `.class`) files of the third-party libraries used by your plugin. You can use as many external libraries as you want, as long as you tell your users to download them into that folder. Then your plugin can be installed in the usual way and ImageJ will add that folder to the library path.

Summary

In this chapter, you have learned how to code your own plugins and went through some useful API methods. We also learned how to configure the Eclipse IDE to develop new plugins much more comfortably than just using the native ImageJ editor.

Index

FIJI
  about 101
  URL 102
Fiji Is Not ImageJ. *See* FIJI
File.openDialog(message) function 82
FITS 17
FloatProcessor object 106
for loop 79
Fourier transform 63, 64
frequency domain
  image filtering 65, 66
functions 81

G

Gap between images 18
GenericDialog class 110, 112
getNextNumber() method 111
GIF 17, 23
Google Scholar
  URL 8
GUI
  adding, to plugins 110-112

H

histogram 32-35
Hue, Saturation, Brightness (HSB) 26

I

IEEE Xplore
  URL 8
if (condition) and if (condition)... else
      statements 80
image filtering
  in frequency domain 65, 66
  in spatial domain 53-58
ImageJ
  about 7, 8
  configuration, options 11
  installation, updating 10, 11
  installing 9
  macro 73
  memory limit, increasing 12, 13
  plugins 91
  setting up, under Eclipse IDE 113-117

stable version, URL for downloading 9
  window 10
ImageJ Information and Documentation
      Portal
  URL 14
ImageJ plugin API 112
image overlay 51-53
ImagePlus object 106
ImageProcessor object 106, 109
images
  digital image 17
  dimensions, obtaining 83
  online sample images 19
  opened images, finding 82
  opening, from macro 82
  opening, with certain format 15-17
  properties, information text 16
  regions, selecting for 43
  registration 96, 97
  resizing 40, 41
  saving 20
  specific image, selecting 84, 85
  title 16
  zooming in 20, 21
image segmentation 94
installation
  ImageJ 9
  ImageJ, on Linux 10
  ImageJ, on Mac OS 10
  ImageJ, on Windows 9, 10
  updating 10, 11

J

Java
  URL 9
Java Runtime Environment. *See* Java
jClustering
  URL 96
JPG 17

L

Laboratory for Optical and Computational
      Instrumentation (LOCI) 94
lines 44, 47

STACK_REQUIRED constant 108
stacks 27-32

T

thresholding 38, 39
TIFF 17
trainable Weka segmentation
  URL 95
Transfer Function 99

V

variables 77, 78
var keyword 89
Volume Viewer 99, 100
voxel 26

W

while loop 80
Windows
  ImageJ, installing 9, 10

Thank you for buying
Image Processing with Imagej

About Packt Publishing

Packt, pronounced 'packed', published its first book "*Mastering phpMyAdmin for Effective MySQL Management*" in April 2004 and subsequently continued to specialize in publishing highly focused books on specific technologies and solutions.

Our books and publications share the experiences of your fellow IT professionals in adapting and customizing today's systems, applications, and frameworks. Our solution based books give you the knowledge and power to customize the software and technologies you're using to get the job done. Packt books are more specific and less general than the IT books you have seen in the past. Our unique business model allows us to bring you more focused information, giving you more of what you need to know, and less of what you don't.

Packt is a modern, yet unique publishing company, which focuses on producing quality, cutting-edge books for communities of developers, administrators, and newbies alike. For more information, please visit our website: www.packtpub.com.

About Packt Open Source

In 2010, Packt launched two new brands, Packt Open Source and Packt Enterprise, in order to continue its focus on specialization. This book is part of the Packt Open Source brand, home to books published on software built around Open Source licences, and offering information to anybody from advanced developers to budding web designers. The Open Source brand also runs Packt's Open Source Royalty Scheme, by which Packt gives a royalty to each Open Source project about whose software a book is sold.

Writing for Packt

We welcome all inquiries from people who are interested in authoring. Book proposals should be sent to author@packtpub.com. If your book idea is still at an early stage and you would like to discuss it first before writing a formal book proposal, contact us; one of our commissioning editors will get in touch with you.

We're not just looking for published authors; if you have strong technical skills but no writing experience, our experienced editors can help you develop a writing career, or simply get some additional reward for your expertise.

OpenCV Computer Vision with Python

ISBN: 978-1-78216-392-3   Paperback: 122 pages

Learn to capture videos, manipulate images, and track objects with Python using the OpenCV Library

1. Set up OpenCV, its Python bindings, and optional Kinect drivers on Windows, Mac or Ubuntu

2. Create an application that tracks and manipulates faces

3. Identify face regions using normal color images and depth images

OpenCV 2 Computer Vision Application Programming Cookbook

ISBN: 978-1-84951-324-1   Paperback: 304 pages

Over 50 recipes to master this library of programming functions for real-time computer version

1. Teaches you how to program computer vision applications in C++ using the different features of the OpenCV library

2. Demonstrates the important structures and functions of OpenCV in detail with complete working examples

3. Describes fundamental concepts in computer vision and image processing

Please check **www.PacktPub.com** for information on our titles

MATLAB Graphics and Data Visualization Cookbook

ISBN: 978-1-84969-316-5   Paperback: 284 pages

Tell data stories with compelling graphics using this collection of data visualization recipes

1. Collection of data visualization recipes with functionalized versions of common tasks for easy integration into your data analysis workflow

2. Recipes cross-referenced with MATLAB product pages and MATLAB Central File Exchange resources for improved coverage

3. Includes hand created indices to find exactly what you need; such as application driven, or functionality driven solutions

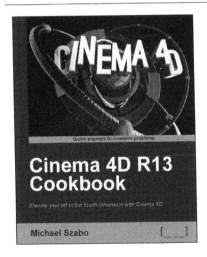

Cinema 4D R13 Cookbook

ISBN: 978-1-84969-186-4   Paperback: 514 pages

Elevate your art to the fourth dimension with Cinema 4D

1. Master all the important aspects of Cinema 4D

2. Learn how real-world knowledge of cameras and lighting translates onto a 3D canvas

3. Learn Advanced features like Mograph, Xpresso, and Dynamics

4. Become an advanced Cinema 4D user with concise and effective recipes

Please check **www.PacktPub.com** for information on our titles

Made in the USA
Lexington, KY
30 August 2018